Love
+
Work

Love
+
Work

How to find
what you love,
love what you do,
and do it for
the rest of
your life

Marcus Buckingham

HARVARD BUSINESS REVIEW PRESS
Boston, Massachusetts

Copyright 2022 One Thing Productions, Inc.

All rights reserved

Printed in the United States of America

10 9 8 7 6 5 4 3 2 1

The web addresses referenced in this book were live and correct at the time of the book's publication but may be subject to change.

Library of Congress Cataloging-in-Publication Data
Names: Buckingham, Marcus, author.
   Title: Love + work : how to find what you love, love what you do, and do it
       for the rest of your life / Marcus Buckingham.
   Other titles: Love plus work : how to find what you love, love what you do,
       and do it for the rest of your life
   Description: Boston, MA : Harvard Business Review Press, [2022] | Includes
       index.
   Identifiers: LCCN 2021046618 (print) | LCCN 2021046619 (ebook) |
       ISBN 9781647821234 (hardback) | ISBN 9781647821241 (epub)
   Subjects: LCSH: Employee motivation. | Job satisfaction. | Love. |
       Work—Psychological aspects.
   Classification: LCC HF5549.5.M63 B827 2022 (print) |
       LCC HF5549.5.M63 (ebook) | DDC 658.3/14—dc23/eng/20211108
   LC record available at https://lccn.loc.gov/2021046618
   LC ebook record available at https://lccn.loc.gov/2021046619
   ISBN: 978-1-64782-123-4
   eISBN: 978-1-64782-124-1

The paper used in this publication meets the requirements of the American National Standard for Permanence of Paper for Publications and Documents in Libraries and Archives Z39.48-1992.

To Myshel, for it all, with love.

And when you work with love

you bind your self to yourself,

and to one another,

and to God . . .

Work is love made visible.

—Kahlil Gibran, *The Prophet*

Contents

Part Two

Seven Devils

(You'll Meet along the Way, and How to Outwit Them)

Part Three

Make Love + Work Come Alive

Introductions

Hi. I'm Marcus Buckingham and it's lovely to meet you. I read magazines backwards. And with books, I read the last page first.

Maybe you do the same. If you do, then you already know that this book ends with the same ten words it starts with. Well, nine, actually. I drop the "Buckingham" because I figure by the end, you and me, we'll be on a first-name basis. But surname aside, the start and the end are the same.

Introductions are funny, aren't they? You don't know me. I don't know you. We say hi, nod, shake, and introduce ourselves. The word "introduction" comes from the Latin verb *introducere*, meaning *to lead in.* This leading in assumes that the parties involved will go deeper and learn more about one another. Otherwise, what would be the point of the introduction, right?

What if I told you that you don't know yourself enough to have any kind of authentic relationship with yourself beyond that "lead in."

It's not your fault.

How many years of math did you take? Science? Social studies? What about Spanish or French?

And how many years did you spend learning about you?

No years, I bet.

Months? Nope.

What about a week? Have you ever spent a week diving into the extraordinary uniqueness of you?

Two years ago I was speaking at a large leadership conference. It was a group of spa owners and operators. Mostly women, as it happens. A smart, fun group.

I said the math, science, Spanish thing and then asked, "When was the last time you spent any time studying the uniqueness of you?"

A pause. There's always a pause. And straight faces, stares. But this time a woman about ten rows in yells: "I took your StrengthsFinder assessment!"

People chuckled, cheered. Takes courage to yell out in a room of a thousand. I asked her to stand.

"What's your name?"

"Destiny," she said.

"Brittney?"

"No, DESTINY," she said louder.

I had erred on purpose. "Hi, Destiny . . . how long did the assessment take?"

"About twenty minutes," she answered.

"How about the results report? How long did that take you to read?"

"About fifteen minutes," she shrugged.

"OK, great. And where is your report now?"

"Uhhhh . . . I put it in my desk drawer, I think?" Her pitch rising at the end.

"So thirty-five minutes. Only thirty-five minutes on you, Destiny?"

A pause.

"Well . . . does therapy count?" she said with the biggest, best belly laugh. The crowd roared around her.

I cocreated the StrengthsFinder system with Don Clifton in 2001. Then the StandOut assessment exactly a decade later. I've done research and given thousands of speeches in just about every country. It doesn't seem to matter your gender, age, race, religion, nationality, culture—people around the world don't spend much time at all learning about who they are at their very best.

And, of course, since they're so close to those things they love to do, they don't value them. I imagine the same'll be true for you. We see just how easy it is for you to remember customers, their names, and something distinct about them, and we marvel at this gift. We see you zero in instinctively on that one error in the long lines of computer code, and we're amazed. We watch as you find just the right words, tone, and eye contact to calm that patient down, and we wish we could be so naturally reassuring. You? You aren't astounded by these gifts. You are inside them, so interwoven with them that it's not just that you don't value them. It's more that you don't see them at all.

You can go a lifetime never seeing them.

Tragically, most of us do.

And Destiny, if you're reading, a) I'll never forget your laugh. It still makes me happy. And b) No, therapy doesn't count. Because the focus in therapy is typically on what's *wrong* with you. And the work in therapy? How to fix what's wrong.

Us humans, we're masters at drilling into what's wrong with us. From the beginning of your existence, the word you heard most from your parents was "No" or "Don't." Your parents' job was to keep you alive. They meant well. You got really good at understanding all the bad things around you. Hot stove, busy street, granny's rosary.

Then you go to school. You get an A+ in drawing and painting and a C– in math. Nobody talks about your love for the arts. Everyone's attention is on your flailing in math.

Then you go to work and have your first performance review. The first thirteen minutes are delightful, and the other forty-seven are spent on your "areas of opportunities" and a plan for your "development."

Then you get married and go to therapy.

The uncomfortable truth is that, more than likely, no one is worrying about what makes you unique. Nobody is dedicated to introducing you to yourself, to helping you get curious about and build a really deep relationship with you at your best. School doesn't do it: schools want to make sure that everybody learns what everybody is supposed to learn. Work doesn't do it: work is most concerned about performance, about what needs to get done. Everybody in your life, since childhood, has had expectations and demands that don't necessarily have any direct connection to you discovering the unique things you love and building a life around them.

Of course, your parents want you to be happy. But if you told them that living in your van and selling burritos to hungry surfers is what makes you happy, I think they'd start pointing to alternative, more "successful" paths.

What no one is doing is starting with you, listening to you, paying attention to what you instinctively pay attention to, and giving you methods and techniques to then apply these unique gifts in the world. Which is a problem for you since, as Steve Jobs said in his famous Stanford commencement address, "The only way to do great work is to love what you do."

Well, yes, that's an easy thing to agree with—who wouldn't want a life in which you get to find those things you love and then turn them into a contribution so valuable that people will actually pay you to do what you love? And it's an easy thing to say to anyone just starting out in their career, or thinking about a career change. It just rolls off the tongue, doesn't it. "Find what you love, and do it!"

The hard part is the doing. Of course, you want a life in which you get to do a lot of what you love. You have within you so much energy, so much insight, so much power, so much joy. You don't want to get to the end of your life and look back and realize that you didn't get to feel any of it. You want to get to the end and look back and know—deep in the very heart of you—that no matter how much money you made or didn't make, you lived a first-rate version of your very own life, rather than a second-rate version of somebody else's.

But how do you actually do it?

The data on this is a bit confusing, to be honest. Survey the most successful, most resilient, and most engaged doctors, teachers, entrepreneurs—really, anyone who's thriving in any profession whatsoever—and the number of people who self-report that they love *all* they do is tiny. So to tell you that to thrive in your life you've got to "do what you love" would seem to be setting you up for failure.

And yet, dig a little further in, and Steve Jobs was still right. To do anything great in your life, you will have to take seriously what you love and express it in some sort of productive way. We know this because when we survey a group of people who are highly successful, resilient, and engaged and a contrast group of people who are less so, the two best questions to separate them are these:

- Do you have a chance to play to your strengths every day?

- Were you excited to go to work every day last week?

Those people who are thriving answer "strongly agree" to both of these. Every single day they report that they get to do something that plays to the best of themselves, something that gets them excited. Not all day. Not everything. Just some things—but every day. They don't necessarily "do all they love." Instead, they find the love in what they do. Every day.

You *can* learn to do what all these thriving people do. You *can* learn how they did it, and apply this to all parts of your own life. You don't necessarily need to hold out for that perfect job where you do all that you love. Instead, you can learn the skill of finding the love in what you do. You can learn to identify those activities that excite you, where you feel at ease, at your best, pinpoint those moments or situations or outcomes that you love, and then learn how to weave them into what you do, every day.[1]

You are the project of this book. Together, you and I are going to uncover the mysteries of you, and reveal to you the unimaginably unique mark you can make on the world. Give yourself more than the thirty-five minutes Destiny did. Take the time to go beyond the introduction, and dive into the intricacies of what makes you "you." Use the book as your primer so that, over the course of your life, you can stand strong in who you are, and what you love to do, and how you choose to express that love. There is no one, nor will there ever be, who is quite like you. Which activities you love, what draws you in, what keeps your attention, what lifts you up, what drags you down are part of a pattern you share with precisely no one. You deserve a life that reflects this truth. You deserve a story where in school, and at home, and at work, and in your relationships you become expert in how to draw love from life, and how to weave this love into contribution.

You deserve, in all parts of your life, a lifelong love story.

My most personal commitment to you is that this book will help you tell it.

Your Fellow Traveler

You know my name, but not much else. Journeying together all the way to the very heart of you requires that we trust each other. You've spent a good deal of your life trying to fit in and armor yourself against the harsh realities of family, school, and work. So have I. If we're going to free each other of that armor and open ourselves up to more, we'll have to be willing to share—our successes, our fears, our hopes, mistakes, loves.

I confess this isn't easy for me. I'm one of those people who studiously avoid eye contact on planes so that, God forbid, I don't have to get into an actual conversation with the human sitting next to me. But, on this particular journey, distance and separation aren't going to be our friend. We need curiosity, honesty, and—I can't quite bear to say it, but OK—vulnerability.

So, yes, name's Marcus. British. Mum's from a family of coal miners in North Yorkshire. Dad's parents were in retail in the South. He was a Royal Air Force lieutenant. They met on the base. He brought her down South. She was a teacher. He was in human resources.

Relatively happy childhood. Older brother. Younger sister. So yup, I'm the consensus-seeking, peace-making middle child.

Huge and long-suffering Arsenal fan—if you know soccer, you'll understand why.

Huge and long-suffering Nebraska Cornhuskers fan—if you know college football, you'll understand why.

College-educated in the UK, then came over to Lincoln, Nebraska—more later in the book on why the heck I would make such a leap.

By training and by disposition, I am a psychometrician. Meaning I've spent my career finding ways to measure things about you that are important, but that can't be counted.

I can count your height, your grade point average, your salary, how many days of work you missed, how much you sold. But what about your strengths, or how much leadership talent you have, or how engaged you are, or how resilient? This has been my focus for the last thirty years. The first seventeen of them at Gallup, and now as the cohead of the ADP Research Institute, where my team does research around the world on all aspects of human thriving.

There is so much opinion in the air these days, so much content, so many sentences beginning with the words "I think that . . . " And while some of these opinions are worthy, and many well intended, my personal talisman is reliable data. What do we truly know about what all the best leaders have in common? What are the strengths of the most effective teachers? What attitude do all the most successful entrepreneurs cultivate in themselves? The answers to each of these questions are knowable so long as we can measure strengths, talents, and attitudes. Which we can. If we're careful.

So in this book, one of the things I hope to do is bring all this reliable data to bear on you, your life, your work, your thriving. I promise you this book will be the most authoritative deep dive into all that you are, and all you could be. No opinion. No "I think that . . . " Just the facts that we know for sure.

This is my tenth book, and it's going to be quite different from the others. My previous nine were all based only on science, which, as a repressed Brit, and a data-driven repressed Brit to boot, I was more than happy to rely on.

But your life is a story, and if I've served you well, by the end of this book you'll think of your own story in a new way. No matter what challenge or decision you face, you'll have a smarter and more insightful way of making sense of it. A wiser and more loving way to make sense of yourself.

Which means I'm not going to be much help to you if I don't share some of my own story. I've struggled, loved, reached, fallen, reached again. I've made some rule-breaking career decisions—making that leap to Lincoln, Nebraska, in the late '80s and investing all my savings in building a software company are two that spring to mind. I've made some truly rotten decisions—let's leave those for later. I've created those strengths assessments, written books on managers—*First, Break All the Rules* is one—built a career inside a large corporation, left and committed myself to the life of an entrepreneur, sold my company, wrote more books, and rejoined the corporate world. I've run myself, then a team, then several teams, then teams of teams, then back again.

My life is not yours, and, frankly, mine is made far easier than yours might be by my gender, race, and first-world upbringing. Still, if you are to learn from others' real-world experience, then that experience, just like the real world, is going to be idiosyncratic. Mine is the only life experience I can reliably report on, and so in this book I'll share both what I've learned from it and what the data confirms (or refutes).

I do wish we could be sitting next to each other, and I could ask you about your life, your choices, your stories. But a book doesn't give us that. So I'll spill the data, give you some questions you can ask yourself, try to teach you a brand-new language to make sense of you in your world. And I'll tell you some stories from my own life.

My simple hope is that these stories will help you craft your own.

Make Love Work

As the title says, we're going to be talking here about both love *and* work. And really there's no space between the two. Some will tell you not to bring your personal feelings—your loves—to work. The data, however, reveals that the causal arrow pointing the other way is just as strong. How you feel at work—whether your work is uplifting or soul-destroying, whether it fulfills you or empties you out, whether it makes you feel valued or utterly useless—all of it will be experienced most keenly at home, by you and the ones you love.

What you love, who you love, how you love, why you love what you love, and how those you love feel about your loves—all of your love life is the subject of this book. You are not a sectioned being, with one slice of work over here balanced out with one slice of personal life over there. Instead, you are a whole being, unified. You have but one cup, which is either filled with or empty of love. So yes, we will be talking about your love life. Your passions. Your relationships. Your learning. Your childhood. Your kids—if you have them. We will be talking about how love fills your life, and what this love-filled life creates for you, and those you love, and those you lead. We'll be talking about all of it.

And love too is a unified thing. Love is love is love, whether it flows from your work or your charity work or your relationships or your faith or your kids. When you are devoid of it, you are a brittle, broken thing. When you are filled with it, you are a marvel.

You will learn the most only when you vanish into the subject: How can you learn what you love to learn?

You will be resilient only when you find the love in what you do: Which activities lift you up with love?

You will lead others effectively only when they trust that you know and love the best parts of you: What about you do you love enough to lead others with?

You will develop the most only in response to another person: Does this other person see what you love and love what they see?

What happens when you love to do something at which you don't excel? Or when someone you love can't see what you truly love? Or when they see it and wish you didn't love it?

Let's dive into all of these questions. I can't serve up the answers, of course—the intricacies and idiosyncrasies of your life are your own.

But I can teach you the code for how to answer them for yourself. Each morning many of us wake up and put our amor on. We come to see life as something to be withstood, something to get through, unscathed. We block out the noise, march on with our head down, surviving—as an employee, a parent, a student, a partner. The risk in all this, of course, is that we get to the end never really hearing what our life was telling us all along. Never really seeing ourselves for all that we are.

With this book, my hope is that you can change all of this. You can change your relationship with life and your relationship with yourself. Because, in truth, your life is not the clamor to be shut out. It is instead the source of all joy, passion, power, and contribution. Each day, life is sending you thousands of signals revealing where you are at your best, where you're strongest, most creative, most attractive, most special. Each day your life is speaking to you in a language only you can understand.

Together, as you read this book, let's do everything we can to build fluency in your own life's language. Let's help you learn how to decode its signals to discover the extraordinarily powerful truth about you.

Part One

Signs of Love

Where Did the Love Go?

An Epidemic of Lost People

onnie Fitzpatrick is a basketball coach and career counselor at a high school north of Vancouver. He interviews each of his senior students for an hour, during which he asks them a dozen or so open-ended questions. These are not "Where do you want to go to college?" sorts of questions, but instead "Who are you? How do you make decisions? When was the last time a day flew by?" sorts of questions. He has done more than four thousand of these types of interviews with students in grades 8 through 12. They begin each morning at 7:30 and continue one after the other until the school day ends.

According to him, these are his top three findings:

Over the years, even if initially reluctant to be interviewed for an hour, all the students really enjoy the process. Students miss their appointments at school for all manner of things, even things they like, but hardly any miss their appointment with Donnie.

Almost all of them tear up as they answer the questions—something, he says, about having a space where their own truth can surface without being right or wrong releases a flood of emotion.

The ones with the best grades and the most impressive college applications, he tells me, seem to well up the most—these students have done everything the educational system has asked of them, and yet the stress of this has caused many of them to feel most disconnected from their authentic voice.

"Despite thousands of caring and well-meaning educators, something about the way we are doing it," he says, "is causing our high schoolers to lose connection to discovering who they really are."

My version of this losing didn't happen in high school. At twenty-nine I started having panic attacks.

I was working for Gallup and had moved to Orlando to lead the company's relationship with Walt Disney World. The first panic attack hit me when I was out for dinner with a gaggle of Disney execs. They were all lovely people, but as I sat there in a perfectly pleasant steak house in the Contemporary Resort, I started to feel my field of vision narrow. The periphery blurred. I became fixated on the beating of my heart. Pressure. On my chest, mostly, but also all around me. Pressure on time itself—the moments stopped flowing one to the next, and instead each moment stuttered to a halt, and became disconnected from the one following it. I couldn't catch my breath. I was trapped under something heavy, but there was nothing to lift off of me. Just the grinning of my dinner companions. I felt a mad need to run, to shove the table violently away from me and run as fast as I could. Anywhere, I didn't care where, just out of there, out of that airless place. I'd never had this feeling before.

These days everyone seems to know what panic attacks are. They've become part of common parlance because so many of our kids and students are getting them. With so much focus on grades, so much Adderall being prescribed and taken, so much Xanax being offered to counteract the Adderall, it's little wonder we're all becoming expert in the symptoms of anxiety and panic. How they affect the human body. How to treat them, damp them down. Panic attacks are like acne now. Just part of growing up.

But when I got my first one, I wasn't an expert in panic. I just thought I was losing my mind.

I went to my doctor, who told me what had happened to me. "I'm not panicked!" I told him. "At least, I don't feel panicked. I do my job. Do a ton of public speaking. And feel fine about it all."

"Well, that's as may be," he said, "but these are definitely panic attacks. Stress hormones are flooding your body and creating these feelings of intense pressure. After a while, this starts to eat away at you. Your mind wears out. It can't contain all the vigilance. The pressure spills out into all parts of your life, and you start to panic. It's not this one present moment that's panicking you. It's the buildup of your life on edge."

So I started meditating.

Which got me through the worst of it. Me and my mantra— the word "One," said silently, each breath a relief, a release. "One" on a rock. "One" sitting up in bed. "One" with my headphones on as the plane pulls back from the jetway. "One" took the pressure off. I thank God for "One."

And yet "One" was good only for keeping the panic at bay. It didn't do anything to fill me up. It was a mechanism for coping, not flourishing. I was still lost to myself, still empty inside and clueless about how to fill myself with life. So empty that even when the most amazing things happened—building my company, writing books, having Oprah devote an entire show to me and my work—they didn't register as joy. Looking at the picture of Oprah and me hugging post-show, my grinning expression is all surface, a happy mask, strapped on and held in place by the strings pulled taut around my neck. *Who is that guy?* I look at him now and he's not me. His happiness is unconvincing. A happy hollow man.

Sharing this with you feels indulgent—like I'm complaining when I should just be grateful for the blessings in my life. And yet my experience was intense and real and, these days, commonplace.

Across all socioeconomic strata, all regions, all races, we see anxiety causing harm at unprecedented levels. To medicate ourselves and our children, we rely more and more on prescription drugs. High-profile young athletes, such as Naomi Osaka and

Simone Biles, are stepping back to preserve their mental health. For the first time in a century, the average life expectancy in the US is falling, and has been for the last three years. Much of this decrease is being caused by so-called deaths of despair—in other words, deaths caused by the actions we take to soothe our stressed-out lives. The results include such tragedies as suicide, opioid overdoses, liver cirrhosis, and heart disease.

At work, according to the most recent data, less than 16 percent of us are fully engaged, with the rest of us just selling our time and our talent and getting compensated for our trouble. In the worst extremes of always-on, high-stress jobs, such as distribution centers, emergency room nursing, and teaching, incidences of PTSD are higher than they are for veterans returning from war zones. Imagine that. We've created work conditions that are so blind to the needs of each human being that they wind up experiencing more soul-destroying distress than soldiers who've witnessed the killing and harming of other human beings.

We've not done this deliberately, of course, but it has happened nonetheless to millions of us.

Myshel's Journal

Finding your way back to who you really are will be a lifetime's journey, requiring lots of strength to fight off all those forces—sometimes well intentioned, sometimes not—trying to pull you off your path.[1]

But at least it's you you're fighting for. You have some measure of control over your actions and reactions.

What can be far harder is when you see someone you love losing themselves.

Have you had that experience?

You can deal with whatever life throws at you, but when someone you love reveals the pain they're going through, or the abuse they've suffered, you find yourself ambushed by wave upon wave of emotion. Shock, as you try to make sense of what you're hearing. Confusion, as you try to reconcile this past pain with the person sitting in front of you, the person you thought you knew. Rage that this person could be hurt, or could hurt themselves, suffer by themselves, get so lost by themselves, with no one there to help them.

Grief, too, that you can't go back and fix it for them. You want to reach over and squeeze them so tightly that they'll never feel lost again. You want to find that small, broken part of them and piece it back together and show them that it's all right now, that the person deep inside is whole again, happy again. It may even be that they now seem fine with it all—but you find yourself waking up at night, replaying their suffering, weeping silently at 3 a.m. at how desolate they must have felt, how desperately alone.

Myshel is my fiancée. She was a colleague of mine. I'd known her for five years before we started dating. I fell in love with her for reasons too numerous to explain, but back then if you'd have asked me to describe her, I would have used words like *self-assured, joyous, delighted, passionate.* It was only after we'd been together for more than a year that she felt safe enough to reveal her story.

It's not a story of violence. Many, many others have suffered more brutally, as victims of war, displacement, and domestic abuse. Hers is merely a story of loss. Of how with schools and loving parents focused elsewhere, she got so disoriented, so disconnected from herself, so contorted and twisted that after a decade of suffering she was a week, perhaps a month, from dying.

I'm sharing her story not because it's remarkable, but because it isn't. Here's what Myshel wrote in her journal:

———————————

Camp Weird and Camp Normal. Two camps. That's it.

My big sis was the reigning queen of Camp Normal. Sissy was four years older than me. A chatterbox prankster who practically lived in Dolphin shorts. Her long, lean legs sticking out of the blue-and-white candy-striped hot pants, she always seemed to get the attention she was looking for. Her darling face and oversized head were perfectly framed with thick-cut bangs and shiny, long black hair. Animated, gregarious, and confident, she could win anyone over with her charm.

I didn't have bangs or long legs. Or charm of any kind. Not a good talker. Kept quiet and to myself. So, when sissy told me that our good ol' Catholic God put me in Camp Weird, I listened.

I have a great big Portuguese family. My grandmother was one of seven sisters, none of whom spoke much English. And none of us grandkids spoke Portuguese. But understood almost every word. And because I liked to sit under kitchen tables as a kid, I heard a lot of juice.

I wasn't hiding under tables to eavesdrop. It was something that I did instinctively because it felt right, good, and natural. The table—like my oak tree in the yard, a few carefully selected bushes, my small closet, or my pigpen—was one of my secret safe places. A place to disappear into. Enter another world where I was free to dream, to draw, to make. I had been sitting under tables in family kitchens since before I could walk.

And while my Portuguese-to-English translation skills weren't perfect, I quickly learned sitting under tables was not normal. It was weird. As were—according to my Vava and the Aunts—so many things that came naturally to me.

Watching Bob Ross turn a blank canvas into a happy little world: weird.

Wearing the same *Rocky* T-shirt every day and believing I could become a famous boxer: weird.

Staying in my room for hours hand-making clothes out of hay and corn husks: weird.

Wanting to be a hobo every year for Halloween instead of a princess: weird.

Getting anxiety from the smell of popcorn: weird.

Being spellbound by infomercials: weird.

All weird. I remember the day I climbed the old oak tree for advice.

"I'm sick of being invisible. I love sissy but hate her, too. It's not fair that she's seen and I'm not, is it?" I asked the tree.

"Who are you talking to?" my cousin Michael yelled up at me with a look on his face.

"There's nothing wrong with having a tree as a friend," I yelled back. I am a weirdo talking to a tree.

Enough. I climbed down. That night, when everyone was asleep, I rummaged through Mom's craft drawer, grabbed the sharpest scissors, climbed up on the step stool in the bathroom. I could still barely see myself in the mirror. Took a deep breath, and WHACK. I cut bangs.

Five years later, I was captain of the cheerleading team, taking my team to the championships. Just like sissy did. Five years after that, I was Miss May Day Princess. Just like sissy. Five years after that, I'm graduating from San Diego State University. Just like sissy.

The entire family drives down from our little farm town to attend my SDSU graduation. When the ceremony ends, I dash up the stairs to find them. My Vava is wearing a bright white T-shirt that says "Aztec Granny." I give her the biggest hug.

When I turn around to see my mom, she is holding her face. So many tears. *Oh, it must be the honors cord,* I think to myself. *She can see how smart I am, how hard I've worked. Sissy didn't graduate with honors.*

She turns away. I realize these aren't tears of joy.

I haven't seen my family since Christmas. I've quit my so-
rority and am waitressing late at night, working at the Nord-
strom cosmetics counter during the day, and studying like
crazy to keep my a perfect GPA.

And I weigh only seventy-four pounds.

I lost most of my thick Portuguese hair.

I'm wasted away.

And I have disappointed Mom.

The data confirms that what happened to Myshel will happen to many millions of us. Not necessarily the eating dis-
order, but the losing of yourself. Your experiences at home,
and then school, and then work can push your loves further
and further away from you until one day you are unmoored—
fighting the very food on your plate, panicking at the sight of
your smiling work colleagues, bawling your eyes out in front
of a college counselor because he asks a few questions about
you and then simply listens.

To find our way back to those parts of us that get buried
beneath the world and all the other people within it, we need
to lay bare what's causing so many of us to get lost in the first
place. Because this mass losing of self, this epidemic of alienation, isn't happening by accident. It's the inevitable outcome
of a system actively designed to separate you from you.

Lost and Found

"Hey, Dad, what's the difference between a trapezoid and a rectangle?"

"Er . . . "

Sitting with my sixteen-year-old daughter to help her with her geometry, it was clear just how much effort had gone into the curriculum designed to teach her this particular aspect of math. Here she had to parse the similarities between a parallelogram and a rhombus, describe the characteristics of an isosceles as compared with an equilateral triangle, and learn how to calculate the area under a straight line. And then a curved line. It was dauntingly detailed, a yearslong program of precise terms, methods, functions, practices, and conventions.

No one has yet put this sort of thinking and lesson design into those skills that'll help my daughter live her fullest life. All the questions that will wake her up when she's thirty, or that'll wake you up when you're that age—What are her loves? Is she being true to them? How can she channel her loves toward her contribution at work? How can she use what she loves to draw strength from life? How can she explain her loves to her partner without bragging, or see the loves of others without judging?—are missing from her training. In high school. In college. At work.

She's just supposed to figure it out for herself.

Yes, sure, she may hear a Steve Jobsian commencement address, or listen to a compelling podcast, but she'll find nothing that approaches the level of rigor of her geometry class. Which is odd, and for a parent, super-worrying. Just as it is for an employer—the ones who will wind up hiring someone who is close to clueless about how to contribute their very best.

Don't misunderstand. I'm a big fan of geometry. And trigonometry. And statistics. As a researcher by training and disposition—a data nerd—I can never pay enough attention to numbers: which ones are valid, which are reliable, how they can be used to reveal the contours and beauty of life. But a) my daughter isn't me, and b) even if she was, the most detailed math class in the world—or history class, or French, or creative writing, or any other skills class she might take— would be irrelevant to helping her learn how to live out the most fulfilling and productive version of her own life.

Actually, for you—and for my daughter—it's worse than mere irrelevance. These institutions—high school, college, work—are built in such a way as to distract your attention from your unique loves and loathes, and instead convince you that there's nothing enduringly unique about you. They're purpose-built to persuade you that you're an empty vessel, and that your chief challenge in life is to fill this empty vessel with the skills, knowledge, grades, and degrees required to climb to the next rung on the ladder.

More than likely, your life didn't start off this way. You were made with love, and though many of us experience childhood trauma, your parents surely intended for your first years to be love-filled. They gazed at you as a toddler, delighting in your curls, your giggles, your teetering and twirling and dashing and tumbling, and they dreamed of your future. They looked for all that was right and best about you. They saw in their mind's eye the biggest, most beautiful image of you, and they cherished it, holding it so close to their hearts that they ached with love for you and all that you could become. You were the center of their world, the foundation of all morality, all ethics, all joy. You—your unique loves and how they might grow—were the point. And when they asked themselves "Will she be happy? How can I help her? How can I guide her, hold her, comfort her, lift her up when she falls?" they knew that, to all these questions, love was the answer.

Then you got a little older, you went to school, and there it began: love, deliberately drained from your life.

You sat in loveless classrooms where your uniqueness was submerged beneath the relentlessness of standardized testing. Who you were on the inside was subordinated to all that you were required to be from the outside. Learning became merely information transfer and confirmation, where the project was to fill you with facts and skills, and your level of fullness was periodically checked by testing. The best student was the fullest.

At home, your parents too appeared to have been drawn into this loveless world, worrying about the questions of growing up: What percentile was your weight, your height, what grade level were you reading at, how was your emotional intelligence at birthday parties? So many new questions, almost as if your parents were being rated on your ability to be a normal, well-adjusted, ninetieth-percentile child. Through *your* actions, *their* reputations were at risk. Their love for who you really were turned into fear of who you really were, and whether you would measure up. Whether they would measure up.

Then years later, as a college graduate, you were hired by organizations that were equally fixated on how full your "vessel" was and how much fuller—with skills, experiences, credentials—it could be.

Here in the world of work, you were now introduced to:

- Goals imposed on you from above

- Detailed job descriptions that define the required skills for the optimal job candidate

- Feedback tools that give your peers and boss the right to judge you against this list of required skills—and, if you are found to be missing a few of them, that lead to yet more skills training to fill up your vessel

- Performance reviews that measure you against these skills and give you a year-end rating and an individual development plan to record how you need to do better next year

- Career paths that prescribe the few routes you are allowed to use to climb the ladder

- Concepts such as "growth mindset," which seem benign initially, but in essence tell you that there's nothing unique inside your vessel, and that success for you will

come only if you believe that you can pour anything
into your vessel if you have enough "grit" or "deliberate
practice"

None of the above has anything to do with who you are on
the inside. The uniqueness of what you love or loathe is beside
the point. Instead, you are—from school on into the world of
work—assessed against a set of models. You are judged not by
how intelligently you've cultivated your unique loves, but by
how closely you've matched the models.

So, in truth, you won't just get lost. You'll get hidden—and
by the very institutions that are supposed to reveal you. Little
wonder we're facing such an epidemic of lost people.

Loves Labor Lost

Why do they do this? Why do schools and workplaces not take
your loves seriously? Why do they not make a point of teaching you your own love language, and helping you turn your
loves into contribution? Why do they instead push you to a
place where you are cut off from yourself? Why do they subject you to this sort of relentless pressure to conform? Why
do they not start with you, the individual, and then follow
you down through all the doorways and hallways and secret
passages of your unique loves and loathes?

When Myshel hid under the table so she could indulge
her love of color and pattern, she knew there was something

in this that she loved. Where did this love go? Why wasn't anyone curious about her loves? Why didn't anyone ask her which sorts of patterns she loved the most and why? Why didn't anyone look into the precise detail of her loves and help her see how to begin turning these into a contribution or a learning? Why didn't anyone teach her how to use her daily experience at school, or later at work, to add even more specificity to her loves and what she could make with them?

Why didn't anyone take that approach with Myshel, as they did with the thousands of students in Donnie's class and the school where he works? Why was the one-hour conversation with him the very first time this sort of learning opportunity had been provided—to ask students open-ended questions and listen—not correct, not advise, just listen—to the vividness of their answers?

Were the students shedding tears of relief that someone had finally stopped trying to fill them up and instead was showing curiosity about what was already there? Was it the release of being seen and heard without having to serve up the "right" answer? Or were they tears of sadness and regret that they could no longer remember themselves—what they loved, how they made choices, when was the last time a day flew by?

Our institutions are not doing it maliciously; schools don't *actively* want their students to be alienated and stressed, just as companies don't want their employees to be lost and inauthentic.

They do it—this building of loveless schools and workplaces—because they think they're being pragmatic.

Schools are designed to produce students who can perform well on standardized tests. Workplaces are designed to ensure that everyone in the same role performs it in the same way, so that products and service experiences are all delivered at the same level of quality.

What value does your unique pattern of loves have in a world where the project of school and work is to create uniform outcomes? To the pragmatist, it has zero value. More accurately, it has negative value. Your unique loves are seen as an obstacle to what schools and workplaces are trying to produce. Success, for them, is tightly linked to when they've ground your loves out of you—hence the standardized testing at school, and the prescribed goals, skills, attributes, and career paths at work.

All of which would make so much sense if you were indeed an empty vessel. If your unique pattern of loves and loathes was indeed completely malleable. If you really could acquire any skills or attributes you wanted if you just practiced enough. If the uniqueness of you—which felt so true for you at age eleven—was just a childhood delusion. If growing up really just meant growing out of your loves and replacing them with whatever uniform ones your school or work required.

But, of course, this is all wrong: you are not, nor will you ever be, an empty vessel. No one forced Myshel to sit under that table and draw colors and shapes. Her sister didn't want to do that, and she didn't want Myshel to do it either. Nor did her mother. But Myshel did want to; she felt a need to. And that need never went away.

None of Donnie's students are empty vessels. They authentically share with him because, finally, someone is seeing them. Someone is allowing them to say, "Hey, this is me. I've already got some loves and loathes. Please look at what's inside me. And don't correct me. Don't tell me how to break my patterns. Help me see my patterns. And then, maybe, you can help me know how I can make the most of them."

For me, for Myshel, for those students, for all of us, it hurts so much to be unseen. At its very core, this epidemic of lost students and alienated workers stems from being lied to: you're told your loves aren't real.

Well, it can't continue this way. If teachers are to offer students something more than a shoulder to cry on, if Myshel is to come out from under the table, if you are to step boldly into the very best of who you are, then we must make changes. We must find ways to put love back into our lives— into our schools and our workplaces, our parenting and our relationships.

Each one of us is different. As the Black feminist scholar Kimberlé Crenshaw reminds us, "Treating different things the same can generate as much inequality as treating the same things differently."[2]

She was referring primarily to racial and economic inequality, but her insight applies more broadly. Schools and workplaces that insist on treating all of us the same are sources of oppression. Now is the time to stop this oppression and devise better schools, more intelligent workplaces. It's up to all of us.

And it begins not with these institutions, but with you taking your own loves seriously.

What follows is a road map for how to do that. How to embark on your journey, the names of the devils you'll meet along the way, and the tools you'll need to outwit them. So, saddle up, strap in, and let's go create for you a more powerful, more authentic and more loving way of living.

Your Wyrd

(And You're Amazing)

I s there someone in your life who knew so clearly what they loved but never got the chance to express it? They were blessed with some wonderful gifts, but because of luck or circumstance, never found a way to share these gifts with the world. They lived a good life, perhaps even an affluent one, but it was, in some important ways, a lesser life. Not a waste, to be sure, but a life nonetheless of opportunities not taken, of uniqueness unexpressed. A life half full.

Maybe this person isn't someone in your life. Maybe it's you. You're coasting along, doing fine, the job's manageable, the bank account's relatively healthy, but something's missing. The vinyl record is spinning on the turntable, but the needle isn't touching the grooves. You put in your time at work, but it's the company's time, not your time. You're short-tempered and you don't know why. Your successes at work feel hollow and you don't know why. You find yourself resenting the praise you get at work, the knowledge you gain, even the money you make. You low-key resent it all. And you don't know why.

It's a strangely awful feeling, isn't it. As if you're a passenger in your own life, watching the world slide by, without ever getting out and taking action in it.

And how about the opposite? Is there someone in your life who has held on so tightly to what they loved that nothing—not family, not financial incentives, not setbacks—could pull them off their path?

Michelle Obama was already a successful corporate lawyer when—after confiding to her mom that she hated her job and being told, "Earn your money now, you can be happy later!"—she decided that her passion was public service. She quit her high-paying job and began a career in nonprofits and education.

The actor Ken Jeong was a decade into his career as a physician of internal medicine when he decided that his love of performing comedy was so strong it could no longer be repressed. Now he's known for his role as Mr. Chow in the three *Hangover* films, and he has appeared in a number of other movies and television shows.

Reshma Saujani had carved out a respected and lucrative career in corporate finance, but swerved away from the comforts it offered to devote herself to reducing the gender gap in computing skills. She left her investment firm and founded the nonprofit Girls Who Code.

Madeleine Albright was working at *Encyclopedia Britannica*, raising her two girls, and doing some volunteer work here and there before deciding—perhaps spurred by her master's thesis on the Prague Spring of 1968—that her true love was international relations. She committed her life to this passion, assuming a variety of roles across US presidential administrations until she became the first female secretary of state under Bill Clinton.

Do you have someone in your life who took their loves as seriously as these people did? Can you see what they saw in themselves? Can you see the choices they made, how they figured out ways to use life to fill themselves up rather than wear themselves out? Can you see how they lived such a full life?

Yeah, it's a bit of a mystery, isn't it. Referencing people like this makes living a full life look far easier than it really is. Even if you do know someone who's followed what they loved, it isn't always clear how they did it, nor whether they are an example you can actually follow. Their timing, their choices, and, of course, their specific loves were utterly unique to them, so which parts of their story should you graft onto your own?

To help you find yourself again and thrive in a life that feels fully your own, you're going to need to learn a new language, your love language. As with all new languages, at the outset it'll feel a little odd, like the new vocabulary and grammar are obscuring rather than revealing your world. But after a little practice, quite soon your fluency will pick up and you'll find yourself able to make sense of a great deal that used to be mysterious.

Becoming fluent in your own love language will help you know which choices to lean into and which to avoid. It'll help you mold your existing job so that it calls upon the very best of you. Or describe yourself so clearly in job interviews that you stand out from all the other candidates. Or choose the right role on a team. Or position yourself as a leader in such a way that your followers quickly come to trust in you. Or, on occasion, take stock of your current role and decide that this loveless job is completely wrong for you.

Your First Word

The very first word to learn in this language is *Wyrd*.

It's pronounced the same as *weird* but it's a noun, as in "You have a Wyrd."

And you do. It's an ancient Norse term, the idea that each person is born with a distinct spirit. This spirit is unique to you, and guides you to love some things and loathe others. Having a Wyrd doesn't mean you don't learn and grow during your life. It means simply that you will learn and grow the most when you're in touch with this Wyrd and honor where it leads you.

The concept of a Wyrd was explicitly spiritual. Today we don't need spirituality to confirm the existence of your Wyrd. We now know that your patterns of loves and loathes are created by the clash of your chromosomes—the genes of your parents coming together to produce a network of synapses in your brain that is massively different from anyone else's. The idiosyncratic pattern of your brain is so complex, so minutely filigreed, and so massively extensive that its uniqueness dwarfs anything you might have in common with someone of your same gender, race, or even your family. You have one hundred billion neurons in your brain—which is, yes, a lot— but the true source of your individuality comes from the connections between these neurons.

Here the numbers become mind-blowing. Each neuron reaches out and makes at least a thousand connections with other neurons, which means that, even after your brain has gone through a couple of bouts of synaptic pruning during your childhood, you still wind up with one hundred trillion connections in your brain.

How big a number is that? Since there are approximately four hundred billion stars in the Milky Way galaxy, and there are a thousand billions in one trillion, your brain has more connections within it than five thousand Milky Ways.

This is the true extent of your individuality, the size of your Wyrd. There is no one else in the world—nor has there ever been, nor will there ever be again—who has the same pattern of one hundred trillion connections as you. What you remember, what you forget, what makes you laugh, makes you impatient, makes you angry, what delights you, what scares you, what calms you, what enervates you—it's all part of a pattern you share with precisely no one. As you walk through life, the world you see is seen by you alone. Your reactions to this world are yours alone. Your loves—that action, that interaction, that person's laugh, that confrontation, that walk, that blank canvas, that line of computer code, that perfect color match between two kitchen tiles—are all and only yours.

Linger on this truth. You have galaxies within you. These galaxies will shine brightly for only your life span. And, upon your death, once they shine no more, nothing and no one will ever shine in quite the same way again. It's overwhelming. What a responsibility. What an opportunity. What a gift your loves are to the rest of us.

And yet, faced with having to channel all these loves into contribution, what do we do to help you? Intimidated by the sheer size and complexity of the galaxies within you, we tell you to look away, look outward. We teach you about parallelograms. And grammar, and presidents, and nations. And all the while you feel your loves, your Wyrd, swirling away inside of you, spiraling up and out of you. You can't contain yourself.

Three Things to Know about Your Wyrd

First, your Wyrd is so interwoven into your sense of self, it can be quite tricky to figure out precisely what yours looks like. To discover your Wyrd, trust in your loves. Trust that what you lean into, what makes you happy, what makes you feel in control, what brings you joy—trust that all these little love signs are worth taking seriously, because each one, despite what anyone may tell you, is utterly unique to you.

More than likely you've never heard this, because most of psychology, and social psychology, is intent on putting you—and everyone else—into categories. Thus you are gregarious, while this person over here is shy. You are organized, they are spontaneous. You are competitive, they are altruistic.

This makes the complexity of your Wyrd—those trillions of synaptic connections—easier for others to deal with, but doesn't make it true. You aren't a category. You don't fit into a category, unless we're talking about a category of one.

Myshel has two kids. Both boys. One of them loves to cook but is like the *Peanuts* character Pig-Pen in the kitchen. When he's been cooking, butter seems to have exploded out of the walls, and strawberries have become lodged in the deepest crevices. He's "disorganized," right? Well, no, go up to his room and you'll see his closet is color-coded, and each night before bed he lays out his outfit for the next day. When his older brother walks into the kitchen—whether he's opening a carton of juice or peeling an orange—he goes straight to the sink, puts Purell on his hands, wipes up any residue anywhere in the vicinity, and neatly returns everything to its resting place in the fridge or pantry. So, he's the "conscientious" one, right? Well, again, no, not really. Go up to his room and it's like the towel fairy snuck in and threw up all over it.

You and your Wyrd have this same hard-to-pin-down quality. Your loves—those specific feelings that, in the case of Myshel's kids, cause one to clean up his closet and the other the kitchen—are the best clue to your Wyrd. In the next few chapters you'll learn what someone should have been teaching you your entire life: how to spot the signs of love and use these signs to discover what lies at the heart of you, your Wyrd.

The second thing to know about your Wyrd is it can grow up. It can become a more intelligent, more effective, less defensive version of itself. But what it can't do is change its shape.

The neurobiology of this is that your synaptic network becomes stronger in those areas where it is already strong, and weaker in areas where it is already weak. Although your brain does retain its plasticity throughout your life, it grows more synaptic connections in those areas where you have the most preexisting connections—but those areas where your synapses are less dense wither and become even less dense over time. This is why brain scientists describe your brain's development as creating new buds on existing branches, rather than new branches.

Where you have already displayed some natural ease, appetite, and ability, here you will experience the greatest learning and growth. And where you've struggled, found little love or joy, here you will grow the least.

Sounds obvious, doesn't it. But apparently the brain scientists haven't spoken to your teachers or your managers, because at school and work those areas where you struggle are labeled your "areas of opportunity" or your "areas for development." In fact, the opposite is true. Your weaknesses need to be dealt with, but your instinctive loves are where you'll experience exponential growth.

The third thing to know is your Wyrd is your best guide and resource if there is something about yourself that you desperately want to change. Counterintuitively, the secret to curing your anxiety, or your fear of public speaking, or your impatience lies not in investigating these "weaknesses," identifying their root causes, and working to fix them. Instead, it lies in investigating your loves. Your loves—felt by you in specific activities, situations, contexts, moments—are wise. As we'll see in the next few chapters, your loves are so strong, so specific, and so wise that only they can show you *your* right way to overcome your life's challenges.

So, to thrive in life, begin with this leap of faith: inside of you is a Wyrd, an extraordinarily complex combination of loves and loathes. This combination has the potential to be beautiful and powerful. It is the source of all your success, and your savior when the world seems set against you.

Oh, and one more thing. Though the ancients were wrong about quite a lot—planetary movement, disease theory, the shape of the Earth—they were right about the source of your Wyrd. This Wyrd, this "you-ness," was with you at birth, and was not caused by your experiences growing up.

These days you are told the opposite: that there is no "you" in there, that "you" are merely the sum of your experiences and traumas and the stories you tell yourself about them, and that to flourish in life you must break free of your traumas and tell yourself different stories.

The biological reality is quite different. Yes, your traumas and the stories you tell yourself about them may prevent you from seeing the fullness of you, this Wyrd. And yes, healing yourself of these traumas will help you see your Wyrd more clearly. But traumas are merely a barrier to seeing what's truly there inside of you—they are not the cause nor the creation of it. No matter where you are on your life's journey—you might be just starting college, in the middle of your career, or the CEO of your own company—stand strong in the confidence that you possess inside of you a Wryd that is all and only yours.

In the next few chapters you'll learn how to add detail to your Wyrd. I promise you, yours is worthy and wondrous and capable and weird. Just because no one has yet told you how to find it doesn't mean it's not there to be found.

Work Is for Love, Love Is for Work

Think back for a moment on that someone you know who lived a full life. You get the sense, don't you, that they were on to something. That they had somehow cut through all the noise, and tuned themselves into a signal only they could hear. And they didn't do this in spite of their work. Rather, they seemed to be doing it *through* their work. Their loves and their work were inextricably linked.

In their telling, "work" does not simply mean "job." It is not merely manual or knowledge labor. Instead, "work" is anything of value they created for someone else. Yes, your job—done well—is work. But learning is also work. Supporting a loved one in a relationship is work. Parenting your kids is work. Community activism is work. Sharing your faith is work. Anything of value you offer to others is your work. Your life, lived fully, is the search for the strongest possible connection between what you feel—your loves—and what you give to others—your work.

Here you may think of love and work as antagonists, as the opposite sides of a great divide—as in, love is wild, work is discipline; love is fluid, work is structured; love is ineffable, work is detailed and defined; love is soft, work is tough. But this antagonism doesn't stand up to scrutiny.

When you see someone do something with excellence, there is always love in it—*loveless excellence* is an oxymoron. When someone makes something with love, you can feel the emotion woven into the creation. Food made with love tastes better. Words written with love draw us in more completely. Software coded with love feels and functions differently. I have a hat made with love. I bought it from a chap in Ojai, California. Each year he travels to the rodeos in New Mexico and Oklahoma, and when he sees a cowboy hat that intrigues him, he buys it off the fellow's head, takes it back to Ojai, washes it in nearby Sespe Creek, hangs it to dry on the fence by the creek, and then decorates it with the beads from antique lampshades. It's the oddest process, but once I got him talking about it, he was mesmerizing. Couldn't stop him. Why some hats delight him and some don't. Why the beading matters. Why he's never found a good-looking hat in Nebraska. On and on he went, reveling in sharing the precise intricacies of his art. I can't recall now why Nebraska cowboys wear boring hats, but I do know that when I put my hat on, I smile more.

Love and resilience, love and forgiveness, love and creativity, love and collaboration, they're all connected. All of these profound and profoundly useful outcomes are impossible without love; impostors without love.

When you're in love with another person your brain chemistry changes. We don't yet know the exact biochemical causes of romantic love—it appears to be some combination of oxytocin, dopamine, norepinephrine, and vasopressin. But the research does reveal that when you are doing an activity you love we find the same chemical cocktail in your brain—with the addition of anandamide, which brings you feelings of joy and wonder. Primed by this cocktail you see the world differently. You register other people's emotions more intensely. You remember details more vividly. You perform cognitive tasks faster and better. You are more optimistic, more loyal, more forgiving, and more open to new information and experiences.[1] Research by neurobiologists suggests that these "love chemicals" dysregulate your neocortex, which widens your perspective on yourself and liberates your mind to accept new thoughts and feelings. The work of psychologists such as Barbara Fredrickson, author of *Love 2.0*, shows that, while the evolutionary purpose of fear is to narrow your focus to a few clear choices—fight or flight—the point of love is to create in you such feelings of safety and connection that you broaden your outlook and build your strengths.

You might not need the science, though. You *feel* what love does to you, don't you? When someone cuts in line at airport security, you wave them on. When the customer in front of you rummages through his wallet to find the exact change, you smile—*Don't worry, mate, I've been there.* When you argue with your loved ones, you find it easy to bounce back from the hurt and reach for one another. When a project stalls at work, you're the one to rally the groups and keep going. You are open, accepting, innovative, thoughtful. Love gives you all of these things. Love makes you more.

Your fullest life, then, is one where your loves and your work flow in an infinite loop. The energy of the one fuels the energy of the other. Thus, the only way you'll make a lasting contribution in life is to deeply understand what it is that you love. And the inverse: you'll never live a life you love unless you deeply understand how to contribute to others.

In this sense, the true purpose of your work is to help you discover that which you love: work is *for* love.

And the purpose of love is to help you learn where and how you can contribute: love is *for* work.

4

Love Is Attention

Why Doesn't George Clooney's Sister Act?

I n your journey to the very heart of you, to pinpointing what makes you special and unique, have you ever felt you were different from your brother and sister? Or cousins? Or closest friends?

Of course you have. You haven't merely *felt* it. You know you're different from them. You know you don't laugh at the same jokes, excel at the same subjects, get excited by the same sorts of challenges.

Have you ever wondered why?

You certainly aren't given much in the way of guidance to sort it all out. Both at school and later at work, you're told a great deal about how genders, generations, religions, and races differ, and why you should be respectful of these differences. But what about people whose backgrounds are more similar to yours? What about people who come from exactly the same background as you? Why, despite all these similarities, are you still so different from them?

I was lucky enough to have two amazingly talented siblings. My brother, Neil, showed such promise at the piano that, when he was nine years old, he was removed from the school music classes and handed over to Mr. Cowdroy, a tiny wizard of a man who could teach him how to cultivate his musical gifts.

My sister, Pippa, was equally gifted, but her instrument was dance. At eleven she was offered a place at the Royal Ballet School, which she turned down—"Why would I go do that when they'll make me stop seeing my friends and playing sports?" Good point. So, she stayed in regular school and was happily whacking hockey balls about when, two years later, the Royal Ballet School came back and again tried to recruit her to devote her life to dance—apparently, she had that rare a talent. At which point she relented, and we never saw her again.

Not quite, but off she went to become a professional ballet dancer for twenty years, with all the dedication and discipline that this profession requires.

I displayed no such gifts. My dad was sure I had some, so he kept thrusting instruments into my willing hands. I say "willing" because I would've dearly loved to have had the musical gift. I saw how much attention my brother and sister got, and I wanted some of that. Each Christmas, on Boxing Day, we would put on a von Trapp–like show for our friends and neighbors, with songs and dances created and performed by the Buckingham family. Or rather, the songs were written by my father and performed by my brother, and the dances were choreographed and performed by my sister.

I was given a bowler hat and a trombone and was told to stand in the back—they would let me know when to blow it.

The trombone was the last in a long line of brass instruments pressed upon me by Dad. Cornet, trumpet, French horn—my lips were too full for these little mouthpieces. Euphonium, flugelhorn—my fingers couldn't seem to make sense of the valves. And so to the trombone. No valves, just a slide, and a nice big mouthpiece to fit my nice big mouth. I loved the instrument itself—how it looked on my shoulder, how it sounded when I moved the slide in and out, the fancy-feeling velvet of the case. But, sadly for all in earshot, I couldn't figure out how to use it. In my hands the slide was always more of a danger to those around me than a means to make music. "It's a musical instrument, not a weapon!" cried poor Mr. Todd, my instructor.

I spent a lot of my first decade of life wondering why I was so bad at music. I could read the notes on the page. I could even tell you what the key and tempo markings meant. I just couldn't translate them into music. I tried. I persevered with that darn trombone for more than ten thousand hours. I improved from terrible to merely bad.

Which was frustrating. And confusing. Why had my brother and sister been gifted with fluency in the arts, while I, after all this effort, driven by all this desire, could barely speak a word? I didn't know. I still don't. I still wish I had been given the music gene. If I could come back as anyone in my next life, it would be a combination of my brother and my sister. And David Bowie.

You may have felt same thing. Maybe not the David Bowie part, but the *Why don't I have the same gifts as my closest relatives?* part. *We have the same upbringing, the same gene pool, so why am I so different from them?*

It's strange, isn't it, because no one else seems the least bit interested in giving you a language to talk about it, or a framework with which to understand it. You want to know: *Am I really so different from my sister? If I want to become more like her, or less like her, can I, if I work really hard at it?*

And yet look around you—at home, at school, at work—and none of the books, the lessons, the training programs offer you any answers at all.

The differences of gender, nation, religion, region, sexual orientation, and generation are interesting and important . . . but irrelevant to your question.

Yes, you can learn about someone's background and biography, as though a person's personality is created solely by what happened to them as they grew up. You'll learn how Venus and Serena Williams' father trained them in tennis like a drill sergeant; how Neil Armstrong got his flying license at fifteen, before he'd even passed his driving test; how George Clooney was inspired to become an actor by his famous aunt Rosemary Clooney; and how Oprah found her calling only when she was fired from her news reporting job and "demoted" to hosting a little-watched local talk show.

These kinds of facts are true, but they don't help much with your question of why you're so different from people with virtually the same upbringing as you. To figure that out, you'd need someone to explain why Venus and Serena play tennis so very differently despite sharing the same coach, who taught them exactly the same techniques. Or why Oprah craved the spotlight while her sister, Patricia, had a lifelong dream that lay in the relative obscurity of social work. Or why, while Neil Armstrong was pioneering his way to the moon, his brother, Dean, was intent on becoming a bank manager. Or why George Clooney's sister, Ada, despite having Rosemary as her aunt, became an accountant specializing in payroll.

You are so different from your brother and sister for the same reason that George is so different from Ada, and Venus from Serena: no one has ever had a brain quite like yours. Your galaxy of connections spirals in different directions and angles and ways than everyone else's. So, quiet the well-intended voices of your teachers, your parents, your team leaders, your mentors, and start getting in touch with the unique patterns in your brain.

At its simplest this means start paying attention to what you find yourself paying attention to. Yes, school and work are going to force you to focus on certain subjects and classes, but can you find a way to filter out some of their noise? Can you, instead, catch sight of yourself catching sight of something? Something unprompted by anyone else. Something that you see, that makes you laugh or intrigues you. Something that others, when you describe it to them, may not quite understand. Something that, when you're alone—late at night, early in the morning, walking someplace—you find popping unbidden into your mind.

Watching the Watchers

What captures your attention isn't random. It's part of a pattern. And so, to find your loves, your pattern of attention is the place to begin.

My very first inkling—and at the time, it was barely an inkling, more like a tiny soupçon of an inkling—that I might have been blessed with loves different from my brother's and sister's came when I was nine years old. It was the first sports day at my new school, and all of us boys were kitted out in our white T-shirts, white shorts, and white plimsolls, standing around on the playing fields and watching the action.

Each of us had a colored stripe of ribbon sewn onto the side of our shorts to designate which team we were on. My stripe was purple, which meant I was in a team called Churchill's. I hadn't asked to be placed into this team, and we didn't put on a sorting hat to direct us to one team or another. I was just told that this would be my team for the next five years, and that the chief purpose of the team was to know who to root for during sports day, and, more importantly, who to root against.

Yes, I was told, my best friend may have been placed on Stratton team—red stripe—or Sarnsfield—green stripe—

but from now on I was to cheer only for purple-striped Churchillians. This had seemed quite odd at the outset, but by the time the first sports day came around, our respective loyalties and animosities had been successfully drilled into us.

So, sports day finds me standing around with a group of about thirty boys, some with purple stripes, some with yellow, red, green, blue, all of us watching as the high-jump finals get underway.

When the first boy, a red striper, runs up and leaps, a movement in the circle of boys catches my eye. Several of the boys watching have lifted one leg as the jumper made his leap. I turn back to watch the next competitor, and in my peripheral vision I catch the movement again—several of the boys lift their leg just as the high jumper makes his attempt.

This is strange, I think, and so I turn my attention away from the competitors and toward the boys watching. As each boy runs up to the bar, almost all the boys make some sort of lifting movement with their legs. Almost as if they are willing him over the bar. I've never seen this before. I turn to the boy next to me—Giles Murray, who's on my team—and ask him why he's lifting his leg.

"What?" he replies. "No, I'm not!"

I keep watching him out of the corner of my eye, and he does it again when the next competitor runs up.

"See! You did it again!"

"No, I didn't," he hisses back.

Well, now this is really strange. Giles, who's a good guy and not normally strange at all, is lifting his leg when another boy attempts a jump, and is then denying that he's doing it.

I look back at all the other boys and see that, with each jump attempt, the leg lifting keeps happening. And the leg lifting is not limited to boys on the same team. Greens lift their legs when yellows are jumping; blues do the same even when the jumper's a purple. Some boys just rise up on their tiptoes. Others actually lift one foot completely off the ground. A couple even stick one leg out almost horizontally, as if they were kicking an invisible ball.

I'm entranced.

Later that day, I go around asking some of the older boys why they were lifting their legs during high jump. They tell me to shut up. I ask the gym teacher about the leg lifting. He doesn't tell me to shut up, but he shakes his head in a *No idea what you're talking about* sort of way. I ask my science teacher about it. She thinks I might have been mistaken. I ask Mom, Dad, my brother. I'm fascinated by this bizarre group leg lift. Yet not only does no one have an explanation, no one else seems to share my fascination.

I never got an answer. From anyone. But the phenomenon didn't go away just because no one could explain it to me. Each sports day I would watch the high-jump watchers, and each year I'd see the same unchoreographed routine of involuntary leg lifts. And each year my inkling would strengthen: I am aware of something that others aren't, and for some reason—why, I don't know—I appear to be the only person who's geeking out on it.

Did I know this would be the first fascination of many? That I would use this fascination to fashion a career as a researcher? That I would devote my life to noticing and trying to explain real-world, observed human behavior? That twenty years later an Italian scientist, Giacomo Rizzolatti, and his team would discover the existence of mirror neurons, and that the leg lifting was a manifestation of our instinctive response to mirror the emotions and actions of others? That the leg lifting was, in spite of the school's effort to create team loyalties and animosities, proof of each human's natural empathy for the experiences of another?

No, I didn't know any of these things. All I knew was that I had seen something real, that it delighted and intrigued me, and that no one else seemed to pay attention to it in quite the same way.

In the face of the musical gifts of my siblings, I held on tight to this one small sign of difference.

You can do the same. You'll find yourself laughing at something no one else does, or remembering some detail everyone else forgot, or being mesmerized by the packaging on cereal boxes, or the feeling of salt water on your body, or the distinctions between a toad and a frog.

And when you do, your initial inclination might be to dismiss what you saw in yourself, particularly if no one else saw what you saw or felt what you felt. But try to let these tides of conformity flow past you. To find yourself, as My-shel discovered, stand firm in the truth that your loves are not strange. They are you, your Wyrd, your very essence, the source of all that is special and precious and powerful about you.

Pay attention to what you pay attention to, with confidence and without apology.

And then, to dive deeper into the detail of your loves, look carefully for three signs of love. We'll explore them in the next few chapters.

5

Instinct

Can I Be the King?

Love has many signs, but the first of them—the first one to watch out for on your journey back to the heart of you—is instinct.

When you fall in love with someone, you can't find the words to explain why. You meet them and can't help but notice their black jeans, their unlaced shoes, how their bag seems to be falling off their shoulder as they walk yet never quite does. Your attention draws you in, and you notice more. The way they do silly dog voices, the way they hold their fork, the way they lower their lips to the cup as they drink, the way they always do what they say they will. All these things come together into a set of signals that this person is sending, and for some reason these signals jolt you. Every specific thing about them is heightened. And you're in love.

"But why?" your friend asks you. "The unlaced boots, the fork, the bag, why do you respond to them the way you do?

Why don't they annoy you? Why do you even notice them at all?"

You can't say. *That* you do is instinctive, but *why* you do is unexplainable.

This person happens to be sending out signals that you pick up on, and that resonate with you in a way that delights and intrigues you. Meeting them for the hundredth time feels like the first time. "I don't know," you confess to your friend. "It all just works for me."

This same instinctive response occurs in the face of all moments, activities, and contexts in your life. Each activity, each interaction is emotionally charged, either positive or negative. Each moment hits you, you take it in, and it either lifts you up a little or drags you down a little. No moment leaves you at zero. It's as if your life is sending you signals every day, and you've been wired to love some of these signals and to ignore, or even loathe, loads of others. As with romantic love, these signals that you love are instinctive, individual, and unexplainable.

You walk into a tile store, and it's as if you've walked into a symphony. Every stone, every surface, every pattern seems to be calling out to you, asking you to delight in its fine shadings, its slight variations. It's almost too loud for you, so many voices, so many possibilities, and you think to yourself, *I've never seen so much variety in my entire life!*

Then your sister taps you on the shoulder and says, "Look, we've got fifteen minutes in here. If you could just help me find something that'll go with the sofa, then we'll have plenty of time to hit Target and buy some trash cans."

And you, well, you don't quite know what to say. You're in your own world. Instinctively, you find yourself wanting to stay all day. Whereas your sister's instincts take you both out of the store as fast as possible. She can't see what you see, or feel what you feel.

Or imagine another scenario: you're in the office and you know, you just know, that you have to confront your colleague about what he said to your customer this morning. The meeting had ended quickly, and he'd rushed off somewhere, and so now you're walking through the building trying to find him. "Come on," says your teammate. "It's getting late. Leave it till tomorrow. It can wait."

But it can't. Not in your world. What happened with your customer was wrong, and when you see something wrong, it gnaws at you until you confront the person and make it right. Some people shy away from tough conversations, but for you they aren't tough. They are easy and straightforward, and getting them done energizes you.

Your teammate, confused and annoyed, leaves you as you instinctively go check just one more conference room.

One of the many things you will have to learn on your journey is that no one knows what your instincts are better than you. Someone else can tell you if they liked your tile choices, or if they felt you confronted your colleague effectively. But only you know which activities you're instinctively drawn to, and which ones you aren't. Your life keeps sending hundreds of thousands of signals your way—in the form of actions, people, situations— and you are the sole judge of which of these you can't help but pick up on. You are the wisest person in your world.

Can I Be the King?

Ever since I can remember, I've instinctively volunteered to be onstage. The nativity play put on by our local church was so exciting because each year the neighborhood kids got to audition and then perform for seven whole nights and one matinee during Christmas week. My brother always got the angel Gabriel—those angels had great singing voices, so obviously Neil was a shoo-in. My sister, Pippa, was typecast as Mary—all grace and beauty, elegant arms rocking the baby Jesus ever so gently.

I didn't have a guaranteed role, but I didn't care. Each year I looked forward to the entire audition process, and would start prepping months before the date of the auditions was announced.

Which, in retrospect, is strange, since I never got the part I wanted.

One year I was angling for a king, didn't mind which of the three. I got the apostle Peter instead. The next year, I pinned my hopes on Joseph. I got the donkey. My final year of trying out, inspired by *Jesus Christ Superstar*, I angled for the powerful but morally compromised role of Herod. I got Doubting Thomas.

And when I complained that he wasn't exactly central to the story, the powers that be relented and gave me Judas.

All the characters I went up for—although very different in their motivations and dramatic arcs—had one thing in common: they were all speaking parts.

And all the characters I was given had one thing in common: they were not speaking parts. The closest I ever got to a speaking role was Judas—I had to point my finger at Jesus and shout, "Him!" This was the highlight of my stage work.

And yet despite being disappointed year after year, I couldn't help myself: winter would descend on our little village church and, instinctively, up would go my hand. *This year*, I told myself, *this is the year I get some lines.* And, of course, it wasn't.

At the time, I thought the play's organizers were just being mean—*Can't they just give me one little line?* Now, looking back, I realize that they weren't being mean at all: they were being protective. They were trying to save me from the embarrassment of being onstage in a speaking role . . . and not being able to speak.

You see, since my very first efforts to speak, I had failed to. I had a stutter, or a stammer, as we called it. Not one of those sweet little stutters that makes the listener lean in and smile, but one of those honking afflictions where the first letter of the first word dams the river of thought, bloats it into something large and loud and ugly, where the smile on the listener's lips freezes first into incomprehension, then recognition that something is really wrong, until finally erupting into John Cleese–esque frustration: *Oh, just please SPIT IT OUT!*

On my first day of primary school, when every other kid was worrying about whether they would like their classmates, or make the soccer team, or like their teacher, I used the twelve minutes in the car to try to figure out how I would say my own name. I had spent my life devising tricks to get myself through a conversation: by the age of seven I'd worked out that, though l's and m's would always trip me up, c's could sometimes be substituted by t's, which for some reason were easier to say. And so "c-c-color" become a fluid "tolor," "c-c-cars" sluiced out as "tars."

Proper names, though, were the worst, and my name in particular. Marcus Buckingham, for a stutterer, is freakishly long, designed to stop fluency, dam everything up, leaving me hooked and thrashing on the long line of my own name. And unlike other tricky words that I could find a smoother substitute for, my own name could not be avoided, particularly on the first day of school.

I get out of the car, and Mom hands me off to the older lad welcoming us, who, in all innocence, asks my name. I freeze. "Marcus" becomes one long "Mmmmm," and after about thirty seconds, I give up. Pretending it didn't happen, we both walk quietly into the classroom. The teacher asks the older lad my name.

"I am not quite sure," the lad replies. "He couldn't say."

"He didn't say?" The teacher asks.

"No, he couldn't say."

The teacher looks at me with a confused half-smile and asks my name.

I, now surrounded by fellow students, face now matching my red jumper, try to blurt out "Buckingham," but that too gets stuck and elongated in my throat, and my nickname—"B-b-b-BARKingham"—is coined on that very first day.

This stammer let me down. And others, too. Everyone could see it. Those nice church people were just trying to save me from myself. I kept raising my hand—couldn't help it—and they thought to themselves, *We know better. His instincts are off. He doesn't really want to be stuck on a stage, stammering away. So, we'll deflect. Let him audition, and then give him the donkey and Doubting Thomas. It's the right thing to do.*

Sweet as they were, they were wrong. They didn't know better. It wasn't the right thing to do. My instincts to get up on a stage and try to talk, those instincts turned out to be so prescient and wise that they defined, in the end, the entire course of my life.

The same will prove true for you. You will have some things that you instinctively yearn to do—before you've even tried them, you find your hand going up and your mind leaning in. These instincts are the first sign of love. And they have wisdom within them.

So ask yourself, "What do I find myself instinctively raising my hand for?" Left entirely to your own devices, which activities or situations seem to pull you toward them? Block out all the other voices and demands in your world, and see what your answers are. No matter the answers, they'll be meaningful.

Honor yourself by listening to them.

Flow

Find Your Red Threads

*B*efore you do something, love feels like instinctively wanting to do it.

While you are doing something, love feels different. It feels like time speeding up.

Have you ever noticed how this feeling called "love" does something strange to this reality called "time"? How, when you are in love with someone, time seems to both speed up and slow down, depending on whether you're in the presence of the one you love. Before you're with your lover, time drags and slouches, and each moment stretches out to its very limit. You can't wait, but time makes you wait, and wait, and wait some more, as it slowly inches its way up the ever-steepening hill.

Then, finally, you and your lover are together. Time meets you on the summit . . . and immediately throws itself off, dashing, rushing, rolling down the hill, picking up speed, the hours turning into minutes, the minutes into seconds, the seconds vanishing, and you look up at the clock and your time is up. Your whole day together speeds by in what seems like half an hour.

When you're doing an activity you love, the same thing happens. You get so deeply connected to what you're doing that the moments flow together, smooth, easy, inevitable. You don't experience the activity as a sequence of defined steps, separated from you, outside of you, one taken and completed before the next is taken. Instead, the activity seems to meld with you, and you experience it from the inside out. As if it's a part of you.

It's hard to describe this feeling, but we've all had it. When we are inside an activity we love we are enveloped, so in the moment that we are no longer aware of ourselves. You are not *doing* the activity. You *are* the activity. The late, eminent positive psychologist Mihaly Csikszentmihalyi called this feeling *flow* and said it was the secret to happiness.

Michael Jordan, like most great athletes, used to spend hours watching his game tapes, not to pump himself up—well, not only to pump himself up—but more because when he leaped for that rebound, beat that double-team, sank that three-pointer, he was so deep in the activity itself that he didn't realize he was doing it. Rewatching his own highlight reel was his way of seeing and absorbing himself while in flow.

None of us has Michael's talent, but we all do have certain activities that give us this same feeling—of vanishing into the act, of fluidity, of the steps falling away and time speeding up.

And we all recognize it. We don't necessarily need complex positive psychology theories to identify which specific activities we love. We just need to watch out for when our time flies by. When we and the thing we are doing become one.

Bored of the Rings

Every boy has a choice, so my brother, Neil, told me: you're either a *Lord of the Rings* boy or a Narnia boy. (I'm not sure what choice girls had. My brother never told me.) And if you're a *Lord of the Rings* boy—as he was—then you have to decide if you identify with Aragorn, Boromir, Legolas, or Frodo. Neil was more of an Aragorn. I, apparently, could choose whomever I liked, but probably not Aragorn.

"How will I know?" I asked.

"Oh, you'll know," he said. "Everyone does."

So, I began reading *The Fellowship of the Ring* and waited for the clues to show me who was my spirit guide through Middle-earth.

My problem, which revealed itself about a quarter of the way into the book, was less that I didn't know who to root for, and more that I didn't care for any of them. To be honest, I didn't care *about* any of them. I was bored. By the hobbits, by the Nazgûl, by the people they globbed onto along the way, by the entire mission itself. It just didn't seem terribly interesting. Or important.

"That's OK," Neil assured me. "You're a Narnian."

So, I tried *The Lion, the Witch and the Wardrobe*. Which also failed to grab me at all.

"Don't worry," said Neil. "Try *The Voyage of the Dawn Treader*. Even LOTR lovers love that one."

So I did. And I didn't. Love it, that is. Not any of it. I found the book so put-downable that I didn't even get to the "best bit," where Eustace turns into a dragon.

To Neil, I was a bit of a lost cause. To myself, I was a big disappointment. I was odd: Why didn't I dive into these books and love them the way other kids did? Maybe I just wasn't a reader. If reading was supposed to be fun, and these books were the funnest of the fun books, then, well, that left me outside of the circle, a nonreader.

I sort of stayed that way for the next few years. Yes, I would occasionally try my hand at a little science fiction, and yes, of course, I would read what my school assigned me to read, but reading for pleasure? No, sorry, not for me. I'm just not a reader.

And then *The Discoverers* by Daniel Boorstin landed in my stocking one Christmas morning. I was sixteen at the time and had dispensed with Santa yonks ago, but my young cousins were staying with us, so, with that little thrill of discovery still in me, I got up at 5 a.m. with them and rummaged around in the pillowcase at the end of the bed for my presents. (We were a pillowcase rather than a stocking family. Not sure why. Mom was from North Yorkshire, so maybe people were wearing all the available stockings to keep the cold out.)

In among the oranges, and the Top Trumps playing cards, and the underwear, was a book. A thick book—745 pages thick. I'd never heard of it. Never heard of the author. Not that I thought much about that, as I'd long since resigned myself to the idea that books weren't my thing.

It was now 5:25 a.m. The cousins had ripped open their presents and were telling each other jokes from their joke books. My parents were still asleep. And so, with breakfast a long way off, I opened my new book and started to read.

I don't think I stopped reading the entire day. I was late for breakfast. Snuck the book into church. Missed the Queen's speech, the Morecambe and Wise comedy special, had to be dragged into the living room for the traditional Christmas-night game of charades.

I fully admit that to you—and to many, many other people—Boorstin's book may read like the phone book. But to me it was riveting. It is the story of us human beings as discoverers. It contains no dragons, no talking lions, no dwarves, and no Gollum. Only real men and women grappling with how our world works and how we came to live within it.

I had never realized that the main project of early philosophers was to find out which parts of things stay the same when they grow and which parts change. Today it's obvious to us that a foal will grow only into an adult horse, and no matter what you feed the foal it has zero chance of growing into a bull. But why do we know that? Before we had the benefit of understanding genes, what argument could you make as to why a foal doesn't grow into a bull—other than that no one had seen one do so. After all, a caterpillar encases itself in a very non-caterpillar-like chrysalis, which in turn morphs into an utterly non-chrysalis-shaped butterfly. So why not a foal into a bull?

This sort of stuff may bore you to tears, but me, I was hooked. I had no idea—until I read about it in this book—that Isaac Newton was less interested in gravity than in answering the question "What is white light made of?" I had never even thought about that question, but through this book I could imagine him putting a prism in front of a small crack in the wall of his Cambridge digs, seeing the rainbow fan out on the wall opposite, and suddenly realizing that white light is made up of all the other colors in the spectrum.

I had no idea that while humans had figured out how to measure latitude—how far north or south of the equator you are—two and a half thousand years ago (thank you, Eratosthenes), by 1770 we still hadn't discovered how to measure longitude—how far east or west you'd traveled. And I had no idea why latitude was such a slam dunk, while longitude was a complete mind bender.

In school I didn't particularly care for physics or chemistry, and any classes on philosophy were met with one massive yawn, but this book was different. This was a whole book devoted to thousands of people all asking "Why?" Why does the light of a thunderbolt always precede its sound? Why does a heavy boat float, and when and how can you make it sink? Why do all creation myths around the world have such striking similarities? Why does every human society ritualize death? These questions were, for me, as breathtaking as anything that Frodo might be doing with his ring. They drew me in, and encircled me, and then lifted me up and transported me back to ancient Alexandria, to London during the Great Fire of 1666, to Marie Curie and her fatal laboratory.

I *was* a reader after all. Just not a reader of fiction. What was urgent and intense for me wasn't whether Lord Sauron could be defeated, but rather whether John Harrison, the self-taught watchmaker, could figure out how to measure longitude before yet another fleet of British ships became shipwrecks. And it wasn't merely fiction I wasn't into—I was bored by biographies, and somehow even the most beautifully written historical nonfiction read like a textbook. But any book where the author was trying to peel back the layers of the world, and in particular how we humans move through the world, was almost instantly riveting to me. *Just the Way You Are* by Winifred Gallagher, *The Black Swan* by Nassim Taleb, *How the Mind Works* by Steven Pinker—these (long) books pulled me in, and hours spent reading them whipped by in seconds.

Find Your Red Threads

Did I know that my interest in these sorts of books would guide my career and lead me to leave my home and family for the American Midwest? No, not really. To begin with, my interest was just a sign of something I loved, something not shared by my family or friends, something about me I could hold on to as I tried to figure out how to make myself useful in the world.

You'll have activities like this. Activities where you disappear within them, and time flies by. Think of these as your "red threads." Your life—at school, home, work—is composed of many threads, many different activities, situations, people. Some of these threads are black, white, gray, brown, emotionally meager, a little up, a little down, don't do much to move the needle.

But some of them are red. Red threads are made of a very different material. They appear to be extremely positively charged. You find yourself instinctively wanting to pull on these threads. And when you do, your life feels easier, more natural, time rushes by. These threads are the source of your Wyrd, your uniqueness, felt and then expressed in certain activities.

Not everyone who excels in the same role shares the same red threads. In my interviews with highly successful hotel managers, one front desk supervisor said her reddest thread was solving guest complaints: "It almost sounds strange, I know, but I actually love it when an angry guest marches up to the front desk. I find my brain works faster, my adrenaline pumping, it feels amazing, like I'm on edge, but loving it. Guess I have a superhero complex, right?"

Another person—same role, same company, same level of success—shared this: "My best moments are trying to figure out how to get my team to jell. It's hard because you've got all these different personalities, different schedules, different roles, and somehow I've got to arrange it all so that you've got the right people doing the right things at the right time. Of course, I never get it quite right, but I'm so into it."

And this, from another super-successful manager: "People say I'm never satisfied, but I don't think of it like that. I love taking something that's working and then figuring out newer and better ways of doing things. I get bored so quickly. So if it's new, never been done before, first time, I'm right there. I can't tell you how many times we've redone our team awards, or our guest appreciation programs. I'll never stop."

So, no, your red threads won't tell you in which particular job you will be successful.

Instead, they'll reveal how you—one particular individual—will be most successful in whatever job you happen to choose.

The Red Thread Questionnaire

To help you pick out your own red threads, try asking yourself these "When was the last time . . . ?" questions.

The conventional wisdom tells you that your past behavior is the best predictor of your future behavior. However, importantly, the data reveals something different: your *frequent* past behavior is the best predictor of your *frequent* future behavior.

So, to help you identify your red threads, the trick is to identify your frequent patterns. And the best way to do this

The Red Thread Questionnaire

When was the last time . . .

. . . you lost track of time?

. . . you instinctively volunteered for something?

. . . someone had to tear you away from what you were doing?

. . . you felt completely in control of what you were doing?

. . . you surprised yourself by how well you did?

. . . you were singled out for praise?

. . . you were the only person to notice something?

. . . you found yourself actively looking forward to work?

. . . you came up with a new way of doing things?

. . . you wanted the activity to never end?

is to prompt yourself to think about a time, an instant, when something happened that made you feel a certain way. Because if I prompt you to think of an instant that's specific by time or by person or by situation, and something immediately pops into your mind, the chances are that this instant is not a one-off, but is instead part of a pattern that happens frequently—if something is happening to you frequently then, no matter when I nudged you, a specific instance would pop into your head because this sort of instant, whatever it may be, is happening all the time.

Try to answer each question instantaneously, off the top of your head, as it were. Don't overthink it or intellectualize it. Just come up with the last time you felt each of these ten feelings. You might write down the date or the time, but more important, write down what you were doing. Which activities created in you these specific sorts of experiences?

What you are looking for here are the patterns. I doubt you will list ten different activities. Instead, more than likely, you'll find some overlap between your answers. Perhaps the last time you were singled out for praise was also the last time you lost track of time. Or maybe the last time you came up with a new way of doing things was also the last time you never wanted the activity to end.

Use your emotional reaction to the raw material of your life to pinpoint which activities have these red-thread qualities.

Once you identify these red threads, your challenge will be to weave them into the fabric of your life, both at home and at work. We'll get into how to do that later in the book, but for now please know that you do not need an entire quilt made up of only red threads. You don't need to "do only what you love."

Instead, you need only to find specific loves—red threads— within what you do. Recent research by the Mayo Clinic into the well-being of doctors and nurses reveals that 20 percent is the threshold level: spend at least 20 percent of your time at work doing specific activities you love and you are far less likely to experience burnout. Research by colleagues at the ADP Research Institute reinforces this finding. According to their recent global study of twenty-five thousand workers, if you have a chance to do something you love each and every day (even if you aren't good at it yet), you are 3.6 times more likely to be highly resilient.

So, yes, love matters, but you don't need to love *all* you do. You just need to find the love *in* what you do. And as the Mayo Clinic research reveals, even a little love goes a long, long way.[1]

7

It Just Clicks

Dr. Don, Strengths Finder

On your journey, you'll often bump into people who want to teach you new skills. And typically they'll do this as though there is nothing already there inside you. Before you arrive in the classroom or the training session, someone broke the skill down into steps and then applied a sequence to the steps. Then you are taught the steps and the sequence and encouraged to do "deliberate practice" in order to acquire the new skill.

This approach works, sometimes, and is necessary, sometimes.

But other times when you are introduced to a new skill, it will feel as if you've done it before. You don't need the steps because you find yourself immediately able to do what you're being asked to do. Inside you there appears to be a preexisting set of understandings and reactions—the performance is within you already.

Ignorant of this, ignorant of you, the teacher puts the required steps in front of you in the belief that you need the steps in order to produce the performance.

But you don't. You are the singer—think Adele, Frank Sinatra, Stevie Wonder—who has perfect pitch even though you can't read a note. You are the salesperson who doesn't need to read *How to Win Friends and Influence People*—you were influencing your mom and dad from the crib. You are the team leader who doesn't need leadership skills training—you have always looked over your shoulder and found that folks were following you.

Of course, this doesn't mean that you can't get better with practice. It just means that along the way you will happen upon some activities that come so easily to you, it's as if you've found a shortcut. You pick them up so fast, they feel so natural, that you don't need the steps and the sequence and all those mechanics. You need just one exposure to the skill, and wham, you're off to the races. It just clicks.

This "clicking" may happen very early in life, or further along in your career. Hopefully, you'll try many different activities and roles during the course of your life, but whatever you try, keep your feelings alert for when everything just clicks, when you pick up the new skill faster than you should. It's a sign you've found love. Rapid learning and love, they're linked.

Dr. Don, the Strengths Finder

My hope for you is that you take your loves seriously. That during your journey you keep your senses alert for the three signs of love—instinct, flow, rapid learning—and that you surround yourself with others who believe in what you love. Because when you do, great things will happen for you.

The first company I worked for, fresh out of college, was Gallup. You know it for the Gallup poll. I didn't work for that side of the company—I worked for the side that measured things in the world that were really important but couldn't be counted. Things like how engaged a certain person was at work, or which talents and strengths that person possessed.

The hardest part about this was, well, precisely that: How the heck do you measure something as squishy as a person's level of empathy, or ego, or assertiveness, or competitiveness? The challenge was not only how to define these strengths but, more importantly, how to measure them when the person didn't even know if they had them or not.

The master at figuring this all out was Dr. Donald O. Clifton, who was Gallup's chairman and chief scientist. During my first few years at Gallup, I would catch sight of him late at night in his office, him and one other senior scientist almost buried beneath stacks upon stacks of computer printouts from an SAS analytics program. I would see Don leaf through these towering piles, pencil in hand, bald head bent low over each page. Very occasionally, he would take out his red ballpoint pen and circle something on a page, mark something in his notebook, and then continue his search.

There was nothing I wanted more than to be in that room with him. Because what he was doing was magic. He was figuring out which question should go with which answer to measure which strength. To measure a strength such as empathy, you begin by experimenting with hundreds of different questions and possible answers; then you ask the questions of thousands of different people; then you code the responses you get back—a + for when you hear the answer you want, and a 0 for when you don't; then you track the behavior of each person to see whether they do empathy-like things— for example, if the interviewees are nurses, whether some of them give less-painful injections than others, as measured by patient pain ratings.

You keep any question/answer combo that predicts the outcome you are looking for, and you ditch—or tweak and retest—all the rest. Even if you love a question/answer combo and are convinced that it measures empathy, if it doesn't predict empathy-like behaviors, you have to throw it out.

This is what Don was doing—poring over thousands of question/answer combos and examining the statistics associated with each to see which combos worked and which didn't. And he was a genius at it. At both parts of it: the question/answer combo part, and the statistical analysis part. He was a professor of both psychology and math, but so were countless others; none but him possessed this gift for finding just the right combos for measuring a person's natural strengths.

He discovered not only that "How do you know you are doing a good job of listening?" is one of the best questions to measure empathy, but, more importantly, that the answer spontaneously given only by highly empathic people is "When the other person keeps talking"—the empath instinctively leans into the other person's words. Think of all the possible answers to the question "How do you know you're doing a good job of listening?" and you start to realize what a talent it is to come up with that answer—"If the other person keeps talking"—and then to see the proof in the data that *only* high-empathy people, independent of race, gender, or age, answer this way.

The trick here was not to find the "right" answer. Instead, it was to find just the right wording of the question—called the *stem*—to generate an answer that only people with that particular strength would come up with. And then to prove, through stats, that this question did indeed predict how certain people would behave.

Your Wyrd and mine are different, so this stuff may not be a red thread of yours—but boy, was it one of mine. The very idea that you could devise a question that, unbeknownst to the person, could cut through their age, gender, race, and educational level and spark in them something revealing about who they were and how they would behave—wow, I just thought that was brilliant. I couldn't wait to get into that room with him and pore over those stacks of printouts.

I was told, though, that it was reserved for only the most senior scientists. That it would take years before I would be allowed in, and still more years before I would have learned enough of the skills of question/answer combo development to be allowed to participate. That day was what I held onto during those long winter nights after college when I was far from home, far from friends and London and all that was familiar to me, when I was questioning why the heck I had upped sticks and hightailed it to Lincoln, Nebraska. The day when I could sit with Don and work magic with questions and stats, that was my talisman. I didn't care how long it took to learn the skills required. I would wait.

When that day finally came, it was a revelation. I didn't know what utility analysis was, had never done either a concurrent or a predictive validity study, had never worked with that SAS program before, but somehow I knew immediately what the numbers meant. I knew which ones were red herrings and which ones signified something meaningful; which ones would wash out a question/answer combo, and which ones marked the trail to a discovery.

And it was the same with the wording of the question/answer combos. Why is "Are you an overachiever or an underachiever?" a great question, but "Do you feel a need to achieve something every day?" virtually useless? Why is "What kind of manager do you like to work for?" a great question, but only if the desired answer is "I don't"? In plain English, I can't tell you. All I can say is that I knew instinctively that they were indeed powerful question/answer combos, and that the SAS stats consistently proved this out.

The whole thing—the interlacing of math and psychology and linguistics—just clicked for me. Instantly. I saw it. Don saw it. We all saw it. I can't explain it, but it was like the understandings were already there within me.

Don didn't question it. Instead, he just trusted it, and so I spent the next ten years at his feet, devising questions, noodling answers, and then scouring the reams of stats for those telltale signs of that perfect, revelatory combo.

Dr. Don, for your genius, for your willingness to trust in the rapid learning of a jumped-up novice Brit, for your belief in love, I am forever in your debt.

There are nine billion love languages. As many as there are people alive today. Your journey toward building a full life, a Wyrd life, your life, begins with you learning your own. Learn to read the signs in your own life. Learn to honor your instincts, to pay attention when you vanish into an activity and time flies by, or when it all clicks for you as if you've done it before.

Life is sending you signals every single day. Pick up on them, take them seriously, and use them to navigate through the blind, bland, and well-intended chatter of your fellow travelers. Let your loves be your guide.

8

Love Lives in the Details

Does It Matter If . . .?

Everybody knows that love lies in the little things.

You don't love "books"—you love *this* kind of book, written by *this* specific author.

You don't love "food," you don't even love "Mexican food"— you love al pastor tacos with no cilantro, and the best in the world are made by that hole-in-the-wall taco stand on the main street of Encinitas.

You don't love "people"—you love this particular person, because of their crooked smile after they make that self-deprecating joke about their singing voice, because they can really wear a suit, because their whistling when they're content reminds you of a cat's purr. The details, when it comes to love, they're just everything. We all know this. We've all felt this.

So why the heck do we forget this when it comes to which activities or situations or behaviors we love? Why do we make do with generalizations?

"She just loves a challenge!" someone's parents say proudly.

Really? Does it matter what sort of challenge? Does she love *all* challenges, or only those where she feels super-prepared? Or maybe it's the opposite—maybe she loves only challenges where she has to react instinctively, and where, if she fails, she can console herself with the fact that she wasn't actually expected to prevail.

Which is it? They're totally different, and would lead her and her parents to set her up in completely different ways.

"He's so good with people!" a boss writes in someone's performance review.

Really? Which kind of people? Is he "so good" with people he doesn't know yet and has to win over? Or "so good" at building deep trust with those he's already acquainted with?

And how about a verb? What precisely is he doing with these people he's so good with? Is he so good at selling to them, or teaching them, or calming them, or making them laugh, or remembering their names, or inspiring them? Each of these is starkly different from the others. Which is it with him?

One of the chief causes of our epidemic of anxiety and alienation is that both schools and workplaces appear impatient with, and deeply uninterested in, these sorts of details. They rely instead on the comfort of generalizations. All boys are like this, all girls are like that. All English people are like this, all Pakistanis like that. All salespeople want to get paid on commission, all customer service people don't. All engineers are socially awkward, all nurses are instinctively empathetic. All teachers are warm, all administrators are pragmatic.

Of course, none of this is so. One Pakistani woman in software sales is very different in what she loves about herself, her activities, and her interactions with people than another Pakistani woman on the sales team. Yes, they are being paid to achieve the same outcomes—sales—but how they do it and which bits of it they love the most vary significantly between them.

The goal of school and work—and parents—should be to help very different people put ever-increasing detail to the specificity of their loves and loathes, what strengthens them and what depletes them. For each of them, these details will lead to greater fulfillment and agency, yes, but also performance and resilience. These details are love's raw material.

How to Write a Love Note

Since school and work—and parents—can't be counted on to take your details seriously, it will fall to you to watch out closely for the fine shadings of what you love. One simple way to do this is to write for yourself a love note. Begin with the phrase "I love it when . . . " and then complete the sentence. The key to doing this effectively, with detail, is to ask yourself five "Does it matter?" questions.

For example, if your sentence is "I love it when I am helping people," then ask yourself:

Does it matter who the people are?

Does it matter when you help them?

Does it matter why you're helping them?

Does it matter what you're helping them with?

Does it matter how you're helping them?

With each question, your statement will become just that little bit more precise. Not that this statement is permanent—you might come up with a different set of details next year or the year after—but for right now, the focus is on pushing you to name, claim, and understand the detail of your loves. Because there, in the detail, lives agency. There, in the detail, you can find yourself.

I was working with the career counselor Donnie Fitzpatrick, from chapter 2, on how to apply this technique to his students. He described how he'd modified it in such a way that even they, at their relatively young age, could start feeling ownership for the detail of their loves. He gave each of his students an empty cardboard box at the beginning of the year. He called this their Voice Box. Here's what he told them:

At the start of the year, each one of you has an empty box. During the course of this year, we're going to do a bunch of stuff that'll cause you to look at yourself and start putting details into your box. You can put books in there, or music, or sports stuff, or video games. Anything you want. You can even write or color on the inside and outside of your box if you'd like.

He told me about his Voice Box idea and asked me to come up and check it out. So on the day I visited he took me to his classroom, and there, piled high on shelves, were scores of boxes. The ones at the bottom were blank inside and out. But as my eyes moved up the shelves, the boxes became ever more colorful and filled with the details of each student's life. The ones on the very top shelf—the boxes of the students furthest along in the class—were daubed with paint and scribbles of sayings and quotes on the outside, and on the inside were full to bursting, like a pillowcase on Christmas morning.

Donnie reached up, pulled one down, carefully moved aside some of the precious items in the box, and extracted a two-by-four piece of card on which the student had written a statement in bright pink Sharpie.

"I love this one," he said. "This is a love note from a student who, before we did this Voice Box activity, would sit silently in the back of the room. That is, if he showed up at all—so many of these kids don't see school as a tool to learn about their uniqueness because we don't go deep enough in framing it that way. Many see it simply as something to endure. It's little wonder that some students can't see the point of school."

"Now they've been given a way to reclaim their voice, to hear it for themselves, and with their voice comes a place, and a mark in the world, and a future. This kid, he's here every day now. Sits right in front."

Donnie turned the card over and showed me what the student had written:

I love it when . . .
> *I'm playing my twelve-string guitar*
>> *A piece I wrote myself*
>>> *To a small group of people*
>>>> *Who I know really well.*

"Did you know he played the guitar?" I ask Donnie.

"Nope, no idea. I still don't even know if he's any good. But do you see the detail?"

"Yes. What do you think it all means?"

"Well, right, I didn't know either. So, I asked him. Apparently, it has to be a twelve-string guitar because the tone is more full, and to him the tone matters a lot. It has to be a piece he wrote himself because otherwise it 'doesn't mean anything.' It has to be a small group of people because otherwise he can't see whether or not his music has touched them. And it has to be people he knows well because he knows they will love him, not judge him."

That's detail. That's love. That's a teacher taking the time and the rigor to help one kid define and own the specifics of what he loves. It might be the first time this kid had his loves taken seriously. Would he become a professional musician? Probably not. Would he develop other loves, with different details, over the course of his life? Probably. But for now, for today, his voice was heard, and he was seen.

If you want to see yourself, if you want to claim your own voice and own your own future, then ask yourself those five "Does it matter?" questions. Don't be satisfied with vague generalities. Really push yourself to land on some telling specifics. Things about you that only you know. Your journey to the heart of you is paved with detail.

The Curious Case of the Stammer in the Chapel

One June morning in 1978—I was twelve years old—I walked by the notice board at school and saw that I was one of only five boys who had been selected to read aloud in chapel before the term ended in early July.

I thought it must be a mistake—of all the boys in my class why would they have picked me?—but it wasn't. There, in headmaster Mr. Pratt's neat blue felt-tip handwriting, was my name under the date, June 12.

I was terrified. And mortified. I couldn't introduce myself, couldn't say my own name, couldn't carry on a normal conversation with another person. How the heck was I going to be able to stand up in front of the entire school and read aloud? The pressure would be so extreme I wouldn't be able to get a single word out. And worse, as I walked numbly back to my classroom, I realized that I wouldn't be able to rely on my synonym trick—substituting a word I could say for one that blocked me—since everyone in the chapel would have the piece in their Bible study books and would notice if I tried to swap out words.

My life at school was over.

The next morning, the chaplain finishes his bit and then calls on me for the reading. I stand up from my spot at the end of the pew, walk to the lectern, and turn to face the school. Everything is moving very slowly. I stare down at the words on the page. I can feel my stammer stare with me, assessing the words, uncoiling.

A big breath in. I gaze over the faces of all the boys, all the teachers, the formality of the occasion and the space, I let out the breath and prepare to speak.

And then, suddenly, somehow, I do. The words come fluently. A warm feeling locates itself in my brain, then all around my head. It feels like a humming, like an unlocking, and the words keep flowing, all the way to the end of the piece. Four hundred people. Not a single stutter.

Well, not quite. I think I bobbled a bit on the word "criticism," but not really in a stutter-y way. It sounded normal, like what a normal kid might do when trying to read aloud in front of the school. I sounded like a normal kid. I was, somehow, a normal kid.

I wish I could tell you what my trick was, but I honestly have no idea what happened. I think it worked precisely because I wasn't trying to beat my stammer with some conscious trick. I just stood up there, saw all the faces, and these very faces, which should have applied intense pressure, did the exact opposite. They released me.

I remember walking back to my pew, kneeling down, and marveling at what happened. I knew I hadn't actually done anything to conquer my stutter—I hadn't overcome it or faced up to it or worked at it. Instead, the situation had worked on *me*—the sight of all those people had created a specific mechanism that had operated on me. I couldn't speak in front of one person, but stand me up in front of four hundred, and those faces staring up at me did something physiological in my brain. That warm feeling in my head was my synapses firing in a way they didn't when I was talking just to one person. And this new firing pattern gave instructions to my vocal chords, and out came fluent speech. The words flowed smoothly, the time whipped by, I disappeared into the act itself—and wow, I just loved it. It was the reddest of red threads.

When it comes to love, the details matter. I couldn't speak to one person. Add three hundred ninety-nine more, and all of a sudden I could.

And this love then served as the integrating point for learning. If I could speak fluently only in front of four hundred people, then why not pretend to myself that I was *always* talking to four hundred people? This strategy sounds perverse—speaking in front of a large group of people is supposed to be a stutterer's worst nightmare, and can be found in

The Red Thread Questionnaire

When was the last time . . .

. . . you lost track of time?

. . . you instinctively volunteered for something?

. . . someone had to tear you away from what you were doing?

. . . you felt completely in control of what you were doing?

. . . you surprised yourself by how well you did?

. . . you were singled out for praise?

. . . you were the only person to notice something?

. . . you found yourself actively looking forward to work?

. . . you came up with a new way of doing things?

. . . you wanted the activity to never end?

precisely zero speech pathology manuals—and yet it worked for me. Each time I tried to talk to a friend in the school-yard and my stammer began to coil itself around my throat,

I would visualize four hundred people, feel the love of this rush through my system, and instantly the stammer would shrivel away, and the words flowed.

My stammer was gone in a week—and in such a permanent way that the next school I went to, and at my college, and at my job, no one even knew I'd ever had one.

Looking back, I realize that I didn't beat my stammer. Instead, I just turned my attention toward something specific that I loved—this detailed red thread—and hung on tight. This thread lifted me up and up as I watched my stammer vanish to nothingness beneath me.

To identify the detail of your red threads, return to the Red Thread Questionnaire one more time.

Your goal is to list at least three activities—although more than three is absolutely fine—where you saw or felt one of the three signs of love: you instinctively volunteer for it; you disappear within it and time rushes by; you feel mastery at it.

Write these activities down and then, for each one, ask yourself those "Does it matter?" questions.

Does it matter *who* you're doing it with?

Does it matter *when* you do this?

Does it matter *why* you're doing this?

Does it matter *what* the focus or the subject is?

Does it matter *how* you're doing it?

Each question will push you for that one additional detail, that one specific characteristic that can transform a colorless thread into something spiritually uplifting. And each answer, each precise detail, will give you power. Through your answers, you'll learn how to use your own loves to identify your reddest threads, so you can then weave them into contribution.

What a gift to give yourself.

Part Two

Seven Devils

(You'll Meet along the Way, and
How to Outwit Them)

As we've traveled together through the first part of the book, I hope you've grown ever more confident that your Wyrd exists, is unique and powerful, and can be revealed by carefully paying attention to the details of your loves. By now, you know that your life is sending you signals all the time, that these signals are seen and felt by you alone, and that, for you to live a life that feels like your own, it's up to you to make sense of and act on these signals.

This is within your power. Yes, no one has taught you how to do this. Yes, school and work seem more interested in teaching you from the outside in, rather than the inside out. But, even so, no one speaks your love language as fluently as you do, and no one but you can choose to pay attention to it. You don't control everything, but, still, you control a lot.

In the last part of the book we'll dive into what you can do to make your loves come alive, and even what choices you can make in your home, school, relationships, and work in order to help others do the same.

Before you get there, though, be careful: on your journey you'll encounter a pack of devils that'll try to tempt you far off your path. These devils may seem friendly. They may make you feel good about yourself. They may even seem wise. But they are devilish nonetheless. Listen to them, follow where they lead, and one day you might find yourself among the lost.

The Devil's Greatest Power

The devil's greatest power—according to the author Catherine Goldstein—is not his evil intent and forked tongue. It is instead that he doesn't know he's the devil. He is, she tells us, so powerful and persuasive precisely because he believes he is a force for good.

The devils you'll meet on your journey have this same quality. Some will appear as worthy and well-intended morsels of advice, perhaps from a new boss or a training class. "You should welcome critical feedback," for example.

Others will float by in the ether, invisible yet tainting the very air you breathe. "Your strengths are what you're good at and your weaknesses are what you're bad at" is one such ethereal devil.

There are devils that have so woven themselves into schools' curriculum that they've become institutionalized. "You'll learn most from your mistakes!"

And there are devils that began life as angels, and then, over time, mutated into something more malign. "Your identity comes solely from those who share your nationality, or religion, or gender" is angelic in its intent, unhealthy in its outcome.

What follows is a guide to the seven most devilish devils you'll meet along the way.

My hope is twofold: First, that you'll come to recognize them when you see them. And second, that you'll learn how to protect yourself when they sidle up, whisper in your ear, and try to lure you into the forest.

9

Group–Think

You Are Not Where You're From

Myshel loves to write. Here's another snippet from her journal. It's her looking back on herself during what turned out to be her devastating college years.

I come from a town named Los Banos. It's a farm town, dairy mostly. I have great friends from LB. My entire Portuguese family settled there and worked the farms and the fields. I love my town.

But I spend my college years denying its existence. In the Mexican restaurant where I wait tables the "Los Banos" sign hangs over the bathrooms. I don't want to hail from the bathrooms. I find myself hiding my town and my family from my friends.

Kelly is my best friend in college. Born and raised in Orange County. We meet in our Advanced Public Speaking class. She saunters into class on the first day. Chic and so-phisticated. Chin-length, super-straight, snow-white hair, in stark contrast to the dark sunglasses that stayed on just a few minutes longer than they should. She wears a pale-pink Chanel flap bag across her high-neck, sleeveless silk blouse. I have never been so close to a designer bag. The cappuc-cino she's holding costs more than the consignment sun-dress I'm wearing.

She has a vibe that's hard to explain. Like she's there, but doesn't have to be.

I am spellbound.

We were inseparable from that day forward, sharing a mutual addiction to food, fashion, and travel. She ate at every restaurant I dreamed of eating at, wore every designer I dreamed of wearing, traveled to every country I dreamed of traveling to. It didn't matter to her that I had nothing and she had everything. She knew who I'd be if I did.

But she didn't really know me. I'd hidden most of that. Which is why it was such an odd decision for me to invite her to "road trip it" north, back to my hometown, for my Tia Dorothy's seventieth birthday.

She jumped at the invite right away. "Yes!" she said. "I love NorCal!"

Crap, I think to myself. *Do I tell her where we're really going? I mean, nobody ever chooses a vacation in the Central Valley. But she's my best friend, so . . .*

I drive us through the LA traffic, over the Grapevine, and drop us down onto the tip of the I-5 corridor, which is that interminable stretch of California interstate transecting the central San Joaquin Valley between LA and the Bay Area. We stop to add water to my overheated old Honda, then switch drivers, and somehow I immediately slip back.

"OK, we're on this highway for the next four hours. It's a perfectly straight road, no curves and only two lanes on each side. First thing you need to know: there'll be a rest stop every 32 miles. That's the only turn you'll ever make. Otherwise just drive straight. On both sides of this long, straight road you're gonna see fields and orchards of cotton, almonds, stone fruits, lots of citrus, potatoes, berries . . . you'll see it all. But the planting systems are weirdly intoxicating and will draw you in. It's literally row after row of either square systems or hexagonal or diagonal or quincunx systems. It's crazy science but actually beautiful art, and you'll get lost in it and could easily end up crashing behind a slow semi-trailer truck . . . "

"Who are you and what have you done with Myshel?" Kelly shouts as she climbs into the driver's seat. "Seriously! You're the girl that teaches me about makeup and the hottest new restaurants downtown, and now you're teaching me about cattle ranches and cotton crops? I'm turning around, girl, we need to get you back."

We continue north. One mile melting into the other.

The sun-soaked orchards flutter past. Old, imperfect red barns watch over freshly plowed fields. Someone inside is making berry jam.

The patterns. I love the patterns. I used to think that the purpose of tractors was to leave their beautiful markings behind for all of us to marvel at. I stare and marvel.

I am ashamed of what I've hidden. I judged where I was from. Thought I *was* that. Thought she would judge that. I've pushed it all the way down, and now my best friend doesn't know me.

She doesn't know that I am intrigued by the ingredients of homemade Portuguese sausage. That I would spend hours picking just the right combination of pork cuttings and giblets.

Or that I was a super-competitive raiser of champion pigs. I could not only pick 'em, but I was so fixated on the details of nutrition and diet regimen that I'd never fail to turn a squirmy little black piglet into the finest at show.

Kelly doesn't know any of this about me. I can barely remember myself.

I stare out the window. Cheeks wet.

"It's the garlic," I tell Kelly. "We're coming up on Gilroy. Garlic capital of the US. We'll be home soon."

Who are you?

You are a girl. You are a boy. You are trans. You are gender nonconforming. You are Catholic, Muslim, Jewish. You are

Reformed. And Spanish. Well, Catalonian. Not Basque. And yes, you're Arabic, Sudanese from way back, so you've been told. You love football, too, but not American football. Only the kicking kind. And only one team: Barcelona! Not a Man United supporter. Not Man City. Barca all the way!

This is who you are. A combination of identity sources— your gender, nationality, race, religion, sexual orientation, your raving fanaticism for this team or that.

And yes, all these sources are valid. Who could deny that your experience of being of a certain race or religion or nationality affects your life significantly, and that the way in which you make sense of this experience becomes woven into your identity.

Myshel was embarrassed by her Los Banos identity and tried to hide it, but you can imagine a world in which she flips this around entirely. A world where she becomes extremely proud of her heritage and wraps her identity up completely within it.

Three of her grandparents came to the US not from the Portuguese mainland, but from the Azores, a small cluster of islands almost a thousand miles into the mid-Atlantic. They are a proudly independent, tough-minded lot, part farmers, part fishermen, part European, part islanders. They are special, these Azoreans, why shouldn't she be proud to be one of them? Of course she should.

We all should be proud of our heritage.

But be careful. Each of these sources of identity is shared by hundreds of thousands of others. You are one of many female Catalonian Barca fans of Sudanese descent, and while you may thrill to the feeling of everyone coming together to cheer on the *Blaugranes* in the Camp Nou, when you're among them you're merely one of the them. One of the crowd. Monolithic, uniform, one voice.

Where in this crowd is your voice? You have language to describe your gender, nationality, race, religion, loyalties. Where is your language to describe the unique loves and loathes that define your Wyrd?

If you don't learn the language of your loves, as so many of us do not, then you may well find yourself reaching toward broad symbols—such as race and religion—to define who you are. And when you do that, you may gain strength from what you share with folks of the same race and religion, but if you stop there, you may cut yourself off from the strength that comes from within. The strength of knowing who you uniquely are, where you find love in the world, and how to turn love into contribution.

This love-strength has more power than group-strength.

Love-strength is self-reliant. No one can threaten this strength, because it is always and only derived from who you are, and there is no one else like you. What someone else loves, and how they turn it into contribution, is interesting and cool and charming and useful, but it has no bearing on what you love. It cannot threaten you.

This love-strength is abundant. You can cherish what you love, cultivate what you love, be proud of what you love, and know that you will never be diminishing anyone else, since no one else can ever be you. By tying your identity to what you love, you are not claiming you're better—or worse—than anyone else. You're claiming only that you're different from anyone else. And they, too, are different from anyone else. Difference, like love, is an infinitely abundant resource.

This love-strength leads to openness and curiosity. Group-strength, by its very definition, banishes others outside the group. While you may remain tolerant of these outsiders, tolerance implies distance, separateness, not empathy or intimacy.

Love-strength begins with you taking your own loves seriously, and being deeply curious about how these loves can be channeled in some helpful or productive way. Of course, the more curious you are about your own loves, the more curious—and respectful—you will be about the loves of others. Since your loves are so interesting and so subtle and so specific, so must the loves of others be.

Out will go generalizations about other races, religions, genders, and fans, to be replaced by questions about the loves of this particular person. And this one. And this.

So be cautious about relying on group-strength as the primary source of your identity. While you may be of a certain race and gender, and have a certain religion, and be from a certain place, and support a certain team, you, yourself, are not any of these things. You are you, and the only you there is.

Find interesting what is most interesting about you.

10

The Excellence Curse

Your Strengths Are Not What You're Good At

S ince you were very young, you have been told that "your strengths are what you're good at and your weaknesses are what you're bad at."

Seems eminently sensible, doesn't it. If you get good grades in a subject, or if you perform really well at a certain sport or instrument, then this is a strength. It's something that might set you apart from others, that might guide you as you think about what to study in college, or what career to choose.

But what happens if you're really good at something that you hate? Or that bores you, or frustrates you, or drags you down? What should you call that?

It's bizarre to call this a "strength" and tell you to make life decisions around it, since it's something that drains the living daylights out of you. And yet this happens all the time. We display excellent performance in something, and then others pick up on this, label it a strength, and tell us to focus on it.

And in so doing—even with the very best of intentions—they wind up hiding us from ourselves.

Because what you should actually call it is a weakness. Properly defined, a "weakness" is any activity that weakens you, even if you're amazing at it.

If, before you do the activity, you find yourself procrastinating, pushing it to the side of the desk, wishing it would fall off and vanish under the filing cabinet, this is a weakness.

If, while you're doing the activity, time seems to slow down, and when it seems like three hours of work must have passed, you look up at the clock and see that barely twenty minutes have inched by, this is a weakness.

If, after you've done the activity, it's clear that you've learned little, and what little learnings you've managed have worn you out, this is a weakness.

Where there's no love, the activity is a weakness—even if you excel at it.

And, of course, a strength, properly defined, is any activity that strengthens you. Anything where you feel one of the signs of love is a strength: before you do it, you instinctively volunteer for it; while you're doing it, time flies by and what seems like five minutes turns out to be an hour; and after you've done it, you discover that you've taken giant leaps of learning.

Even if you aren't quite good at it yet, even if you still have a long way to go before you get good at it, your strengths are activities where you feel the signs of love. Your strengths are your red threads.

This doesn't mean that your strengths have *all* the qualities of a red thread *all* the time. On occasion you may find yourself procrastinating on something, and then feel the time flying by when you actually start doing it. Or perhaps there'll be occasions when you instinctively volunteer for something and discover, to your chagrin, that the doing of it requires more disciplined practice than "rapid learning" would suggest.

These occasions simply mean that you'd be wise to keep alert for any of those three signs of love. Often they are connected, sometimes they aren't, but each of them will always lead you to a greater fluency in your own love language.

If you honor this about yourself, and really noodle on which specific activities have any of these red-thread qualities, you'll make three quite powerful discoveries.

First, you'll learn that while, yes, of course, practice helps you get better at any activity, the real key to success and satisfaction in life lies in identifying which activities you are drawn back to practice over and over again. These red threads—these activities that you love—pull you back to them, so that the practice doesn't feel like something you are deliberately doing, or even something that you're forcing yourself to do. Instead, the practice feels like something you can't stop yourself from doing. Practice is not a conscious discipline, demanding grit and stick-to-itiveness. Instead, seen through the lens of love, practice is an obsession.

Second, you'll discover that these red threads show you your future. Your love for the activity drives repetition, which in turn drives improvement. So, by paying attention to your loves, you'll gain much clearer insight into what you're likely to get really good at. Excellence ceases to be a mystery—is it natural talent, is it nurture, is it luck, is it the coach? And instead, excellence is revealed to be simply a product of you taking your loves seriously. Passion fuels practice fuels performance.

And third, you'll realize that since your strengths are simply activities that you love, activities that strengthen you, by far the best judge of your strengths is you. Other people—your parents, teachers, coaches, managers—can judge your performance. They can weigh in on whether that essay is worth reading, that math problem is correctly solved, that customer is well served. But only you know which activities you love, and which you loathe. You are the sole authority on which activities create in you those signs of love, and which don't. You are the only one you can trust.

If you say that you love the thrill of persuading others to buy what you're selling, then no one can contradict you. Sure, they can say, "Well, I don't think you're explaining your products in enough detail" or "You'll be more persuasive if you listen more than you talk" or "You're not following the company's standard sales script." They can tell you any one of these things, and they have a right to do so.

But what they cannot do is say, "No, you don't love persuading people." Because you know what you love better than anyone else does. You knew it as a young child, and you know it now. The fact that, over the years, others have tried to tell you that your loves aren't real, or relevant, doesn't change the truth that you feel what you feel.

When it comes to your loves, you have all the answers. No one else has any. When it comes to your loves, you are the only genius.

11

Mis-Instinct

What's Really Happening in the Room Where It Happens?

ha," you may hear others cry, "what about *American Idol*? What about all those thousands of people who line up for days in the hope that they will be chosen as the next superstar?" Each of them, in this line of thinking, instinctively volunteers to put themselves up for the audition, and yet clearly many of them lack even the most basic singing ability. Surely they aren't the true geniuses of what their loves are. Surely they need the judges to weigh in on whether their loves are real, or useful, or connected in any way to actual performance. Surely the judges are the ones to tell them who they really are—just as, in the end, your parents, your teachers, and your manager are the ultimate arbiters of truth about you. *You* cannot be trusted; *you* cannot trust yourself. But these well-meaning others, yes, they *can* be trusted. Their perspective on you will reveal the real you. Right?

So, no to all that. And, if you want to live a Love + Work life, this line of thinking is vital for you to unlearn. Other people know nothing of your loves—they know only how they react to your performance. Which is not nothing. But it has nothing to say about what you love and what you don't. You and you alone feel what you feel.

What this does demand of you, though, is that you pay very close attention to the specifics of what you love. Those *American Idol* auditioners, what did they instinctively volunteer for? Did they instinctively love the activity of hours upon hours of solitary voice training? Did they love the memory challenge of learning the lyrics of hundreds of different songs? Did they love the days and days of rehearsals with the musicians and the arrangements?

Or were these activities not the source of their love? Were they instead instinctively drawn to the attention, the fame, the adulation, and the money?

One of the dangers of being told from an early age that our loves aren't real is that we don't examine them closely, and so over time our expertise at pinpointing the true source of our love diminishes to nothing. As a result, we can find ourselves led astray by mis-instincts.

When you instinctively lobby for that promotion only because it comes with a bigger salary, this is a mis-instinct.

When you go for the job simply because it comes with a bigger title, this is a mis-instinct.

When you opt for the posting only because it comes with more prestige, this is a mis-instinct.

For your loves to turn into contribution, pay attention *only* to the specific activities you love, not the outcomes of those activities. Pay attention to *what* you are going to be doing, rather than *why*. "What," in the end, always trumps the "why."

Ask yourself: In this role, *what* precisely will I be paid to do?

Ask yourself: *What* will a regular week in this new role look like?

Ask yourself: *What* will I be doing at 9 a.m. on a normal Wednesday morning, or 3 p.m. on a Friday afternoon?

As part of my ongoing research into excellent performers in various roles, I've posed to the best salespeople this question: "What do you love most about selling?"

Imagine all the possible answers you might hear from salespeople in response to this question.

"I love building trust."

"I love trying to explain the benefits of what I'm offering."

"I love meeting lots of interesting people."

Or the most common: "I love selling things I really believe in. I can't sell anything I don't really believe in."

It turns out that the best salespeople say none of these things. Well, they might *also* say one of these things, but what *all* the best salespeople say is this: "I love the close."

For the best salespeople, the love of the job lies not in why they are selling the product, nor in whom they are selling it to or with. Instead, it lies in the actual activity of the close. Of finally getting someone to do something tangible: sign on the dotted line. In the broadest sense, this activity, of getting another human to commit, is what all the best salespeople love about what they do. Of course, the details matter. They all may love different aspects of it—one may close through persuasion, one through technical competence, one through rapport. But the activity that fills up their every day with love is the activity of getting the close.

Which is interesting if, by the by, you are interested in sales. Because some sales roles will offer you frequent chances to close, such as Wall Street positions, with their hundreds of closes every day. Other roles have a far longer timeframe and far lower frequency for actual closing—go work for a large consulting firm, for example, and it might take you eighteen months to close even one small deal.

And some roles won't give you any chance to close. In pharmaceuticals, for example, a job may be advertised on LinkedIn as "sales," but in reality a pharma sales rep never gets a chance to close anyone. All they will ever be able to do is try to influence physicians enough that, over time, they prescribe slightly more of the salesperson's products than the competitor's.

So, before you take on a new role, focus on the "what" questions. And if you don't know the answers to these questions, then talk to a few folks who are actually in the role, or in the school, or in the class. Probe them to get down to the lowest level possible, to the level of actual activities, and then ask yourself how these activities fit with what you know you love.

Naturally, there'll be times when you'll ask all your questions and still not really know if what you're reaching for is in fact filled with activities you love. When I instinctively wanted to get into the room where Dr. Don was making magic, I'm sure that some of this instinct was fueled by the fact that he was the chairman of the company, and that sitting by his side would confer upon me some measure of specialness. This was clearly a mis-instinct on my part.

Luckily for me, I was surrounded by people who had already been in that room with him, who could tell me in the most vivid detail which activities I should expect to do, and could even give me the chance to try out these activities all by myself on various side projects. It was during these side projects that the true signs of love first emerged for me—I was sucked into the activity of designing question/answer combos, riveted by the data each combo generated, felt hours flitting by like seconds.

In the end, it was these feelings, rather than the allure of prestige, that kept drawing me back to that room, and that fueled my desire to get into it. If you find yourself instinctively yearning to "get into a room," make sure you learn as much as you can about whether you love the activities "in the room where it happens."

And what if I pay super-close attention to the activities I love, and I try to do them, I really try, and I discover that I'm still not very good at them?

Yes, that does occur. To a lot of people who enjoy singing, playing basketball, painting. You love the activity, you feel uplifted when doing it, but you just don't seem to have the capacity to excel at it.

Well, in the world we all live in, we have a word for activities such as this: we call them hobbies. A hobby adds to your happiness and well-being for many reasons, but one of them is most certainly that the activity itself has red-thread-like qualities to it. It is positively charged, it draws you back time and again and makes you feel connected to yourself while you're doing it. On your Love + Work journey, you'll try many different activities, and some of them will become love-giving hobbies for you. They are precious, these activities. They'll bring love into your life, even if you can't ever seem to get good enough at them to warrant turning them into your actual work.

Your life should be an ongoing search for love. Sometimes high performance will flow from your love, and sometimes it won't. But in all cases, more love in your life means a fuller life.

12

Feedbacking

The Road to Hell Is Paved with Other People's Advice

I am so pleased with myself.

My great friend and coauthor of my last book, Ashley Goodall (he's a man, because, well, British), has called me up to ask for my advice about how to record an audiobook, and I have given him the very best nuggets.

See, our book *Nine Lies About Work* is, coincidentally, my ninth book, and so I've got this audiobook-recording thing down.

"It's actually rather a tricky thing to do," I warn him. "They're going to stick you in a recording studio, put all the pages of the book on a music stand, shove a honking microphone in front of your mouth, and then tell you to speak as warmly and as smoothly as you possibly can. Listening to an audiobook is an intimate experience, and so you've got to find a way to modulate your speed and your tone so that you fit snugly into the listener's ear."

I reassure him.

"Don't worry," I say, "I'm a bit of a pro at this. Here's the trick: look over the top of the music stand, catch the eye of the producer through the glass, and then make believe you're just telling them a few fun facts and stories over a drink or a cup of coffee—this way you'll come across as friendly and conversational. Whenever you feel yourself getting lost in the manuscript, return to that mental image of you and the producer having a wee chat, and, Bob's your uncle, you'll breeze through this."

The next day I go into the studio myself to record my half of the book—we're alternating chapters. I use my just-a-chat visualization exercise and the session flies by. They've set aside three days to record my part. I get it all done in one afternoon.

As I said, I'm a pro.

I call Ashley one last time in advance of his sessions the next day, and re-anchor my advice: you're having a drink with the producer. Make eye contact, imagine a beverage of your choice in your hand, let it flow.

I congratulate myself. I've thought something through enough to be able to convey to my friend not just the kind of recording we're after, but also a very specific technique for creating this outcome. Yay me. Coach extraordinaire.

At the end of the next day, Ashley calls. He's done. It's his very first audiobook recording, and what should have taken him four days has whipped by in only one day.

"Wow," I say. "Well done you! Bravo! So, did it work out? The visualization exercise?" I wait for his affirmation, glowing with pride in us both.

"No, 'fraid not," he says. "I walked in and it was initially just as you'd said—music stand, book, honking great microphone. But then when I sat and tried to look at the producer, I couldn't see him around the music stand without craning my neck, which clearly wasn't going to work. And then when I tried to catch his eye he looked right down at the console, and so the whole thing felt completely weird and unnatural."

"Oh! Really? So, er, how come it all worked out for you? They told me that, as a first-time reader, we would probably need to do multiple takes over multiple days."

"Ah, well, see, I stumbled on a trick of my own. As a pianist, I'm used to sight-reading. And the thing about sight-reading is you have to get used to looking four or five bars ahead of what your hands are actually playing, so that you can plan for what's coming next and how you want it to sound."

"Oh," I said.

"So, I started reading, was awkwardly and desperately trying to catch the eye of the producer, who kept looking the other way, and the whole thing was going terribly. Then all of a sudden, I felt a familiar pattern—reading this book out loud was like sight-reading. I needed to be looking four or five words ahead of what my mouth was actually saying, so I could plan for how I wanted it to sound. If I could settle myself into the rhythms of sight-reading, then I should be able to sail through this as though it were a Chopin sonata. So I did. And I did. Sail through it, I mean."

"Oh," I said again.

I wouldn't say I was churlish, but there was definitely a twinge of disappointment. I wasn't the coach I thought I was. Ashley had figured it out for himself, and in a way that was much more natural and authentic for him than any well-intended technique of mine. Of the one thousand possible nuggets of advice I could have given him, "Pretend you are sight-reading a Chopin sonata" would have been one thousand and one. And yet it was the very first tactic on his list.

My advice hadn't freed him. It had smothered him, with me.

You will undoubtedly have similar experiences. Some well-intended person—your dad, perhaps, or your teacher, or your team leader—will want you to do well at something and so will give you the "benefit" of their advice. To stay true to yourself, please do everything in your power to withstand the temptation to do what they say—no matter how smart they might be.

The Golden Rule states that you should treat people as you would like to be treated. While this is tremendously well intended, the problem with the rule is that it presupposes everyone has the same loves you do, and thus that everyone wants to be treated the same way you do. Happily, this isn't true. Ashley's entire approach to doing, thinking, learning, speaking, performing is meaningfully different from mine, and so any advice I gave that worked for me would almost be guaranteed *not* to work for him.

These days you hear a great deal about how you should be open to feedback and advice from others. And yet, for the most part, their feedback or advice will only serve to muddle you up, and distort who you really are and what you can really do.

The only time someone's feedback or advice will prove helpful is when they are correcting a fact you got wrong, or when you missed a predefined step in a rote sequence of steps. On other occasions their feedback and advice is worse than useless. No matter how carefully it is framed, when laid bare what they are really saying to you is, "You would do better at this if only you did it more like I do."

Here it'll be super-helpful for you to draw a distinction between another person's "feedback" and their "reaction." Their feedback—try this, do that—is compromised by the fact that they aren't you and so are incapable of knowing which action or technique will help you—not them—do better. Whenever anyone says, "I have some feedback for you," politely close your ears. You are about to be—well intendedly—smothered.

However, in direct contrast, you should definitely pay attention when someone shares their reaction with you. Their reaction is a much humbler gift. A reaction is not a prescription—it's not saying, "Do more of this, less of that." It is merely a response to something you said or did or wrote. So, if you send an email and the other person says, "I was really confused by this email," that is their reaction, and they are the 100 percent owner of the truth of their reaction. I suppose you could argue with them by saying, "Well, you shouldn't have been confused," but that's just daft, isn't it. The fact is, they *were* confused by your email. Their reaction is real and trumps anything you might say to persuade them that they weren't, in fact, confused.

In the same vein, if someone says, "I found myself bored by your presentation," then you can't really confront them with, "No you weren't!" Because they were. They felt it. And they, not you, are the owner of their feelings.

So, yes, pay close attention to other people's reactions. These reactions will be excellent raw material to help you understand the dent you are making in the world. When someone's reaction wasn't quite what you wanted, honor their reaction and then think through which actions of yours they were reacting to.

Even more important, when someone's reaction was *exactly* what you wanted—they *loved* your call, your email, your presentation, your singing voice—spend a ton of time being curious with them about their reaction. Ask them why they felt the way they did, what worked for them, when they leaned in, what grabbed their attention. You're doing this not to fish for praise, but to learn more and more about who you are when you are at your best. You are using their reaction to what worked to become ever more expert at turning your loves into contribution.

But whatever you do, don't listen to others' feedback and advice. Well, you can listen, just don't act on it. You will always be your most productive and attractive when you're inside your own skin. When you squeeze yourself inside someone else's, you're just plain scary.

13

Fear-Fighting

Make Love to Your Fears

Speaking of scary, what are you frightened of?

I know we're not supposed to be afraid. *What would you do if you weren't afraid?* motivational social media posts asks us, as though our job is to banish fear from our lives.

My problem is that I find myself afraid all the bloody time. Right now, for example, as I sit here to write this, I am afraid of not writing a good enough piece on fear. And whether my son will be safe going back to college. And when I'm going to get another alarming call about my brother's health. And if my mom is going to crack under the pressure of taking care of him.

So many fears, some I'm not so proud of, all boiling away just under the surface.

Am I normal for feeling these fears? Am I somehow failing as a human by admitting that these fears are a constant companion? The internet—and Machiavelli, and Eckhart Tolle, and Marianne Williamson—tells me that the opposite of love is fear. So by living with fears, am I closing myself off to love? To live a full life, a life that allows me to turn my loves into contribution, must I confront my fears and fight them off?

It sure feels like I should. After all, love is the emotion that opens me up to possibilities, whereas fear narrows my mind and my options. And let's face it, there are times when this is no bad thing. Narrowing my focus is precisely what fear is for. It is a survival emotion designed to elevate my heart rate, flood my body with cortisol and adrenaline, and focus my mind only on the perceived threat and whether I should stand and fight, or turn and run for my life. All of which will be invaluable to me if I happen to see a bear emerge from the woods or a bandit jump out from behind a tree.

But if I'm trying to do something more creative, such as deepen a relationship, design a software program, solve a customer's problem, or paint a canvas, then this fear is far less valuable. No one can create in fear.

And yet I find I can't banish fear. It's a part of being a human in the world. Feeling fear is as natural to me as feeling empathy, or joy, or anger. To pretend that it isn't, to try to live without fear, is fakery. Real humans can't do this.

So, what then should we do with our fears? We spend our life fighting them, looking away from them, running away from them, and yet we wake up each morning, and they rise with us.

With fear as our life's companion, the best thing to do is what you would do with any companion: turn and look at them, ask them loads of questions, get curious, get intimate with them, and, in so doing, let them reveal you.

The first thing you may learn is that lots of your fears are focused on other people, and in particular what those other people think of you. This is not a problem. This is as it should be. When someone tells you that you should ignore what other people think of you, that others' opinions of you are none of your business, please push back. You are designed to be concerned about what other people think of you. It's part of what makes you human. The only people who are not concerned about what other people think of them are sociopaths.

So yes, it is wise and good to care about what other people think of you. As we talked about in chapter 12, their *reactions* to you are an important sign of how your loves are playing out in the world. You need to pay attention to their reactions—at least, if you're interested in turning your loves into contribution.

If you are a teacher and your students don't seem to be able to improve their grade with you at the helm, pay attention to that. Their reaction, and what you might be doing to create this reaction, is worth you owning and thinking about.

If you are a software engineer and you hear that most people don't want to iterate on your code because it's hard to follow, then honor this reaction by thinking about how your code might read to them.

If you're in sales and your presentation did not result in a sale, then, sure, you could blame the readiness of the buyer or the quality of your marketing, but keep your mind open to the possibility that the buyer didn't buy because you didn't sell.

However, in all of these scenarios, remember that the other person's reaction is theirs and theirs alone. Their reaction—be it anger, joy, pain, or frustration—to what you said, or made, or did comes from within them. You didn't create this reaction. They did. This reaction is interesting, and important, and valid, and worth noting.

But it is not yours. It is theirs.

The second thing you'll discover is that fear itself is not the thing to be afraid of. It's not fear that causes the problems in your life. It's what fear degrades into when you shun it.

In a relationship, if you fear the other person leaving you, fear degrades into possessiveness, and it's the possessiveness that leads to suffocation.

If you fear the other person cheating on you, fear mutates into jealousy and suspicion, and these evil twins then strangle you both.

If you fear what other people think of your work, fear morphs into safe, formulaic work that pushes no boundaries.

If you fear taking that new job, fear shows up as paralysis, keeping you comfortable and stationary.

Fear that's shunned metastasizes into feelings that are deeply damaging.

By contrast, fear that's examined yields powerful discoveries about you at your best. When you get curious and let fear in, what you realize is that your fears are yet one more sign of what you love. I am afraid to write this piece on fear precisely because I love writing things that can help you, and I so desperately want to be helpful. I am fearful of my mom being able to take care of my brother because I love them both so bloody much. My fears pinpoint my loves.

In this sense, fear is like pain. For the body, the purpose of pain is to yank my attention toward something vital to my health; analgesia, the inability to feel pain, is a condition that, left unaddressed, can kill you. Fear is pain for the psyche. Feel fear and follow it, and it will lead you straight to something or someone you love, to what you are passionate about, to who you care for so very deeply. In this sense, your fear is your wisest and most loving companion. It knows who and what you love—knows it without judgment, without conscious curation, yet so precisely and so urgently that your loves are revealed before you're aware of them, or even before you're prepared to admit them.

Try to change your relationship to your fears. Don't banish them. Don't fight them. Don't turn and face them down. Instead, see whether you can learn to honor your fears—which means listening to them, being curious about them, and admiring them as part of the real you. Do this—gently, generously, kindly—and they will show you what you truly love.

On your journey, you're told to dismiss your fears, to confront your fears, to step outside of your comfort zone. Yet this is all so misleading. Your big choice in life is not "comfort or no comfort." It is "love or no love." When you step into things you love, you *will* feel fear. That's not just OK, it's fundamental. So fundamental, in fact, that if you're doing something and you feel no fear, then you've lost your love.

So, take the path of fear, because the path of fear is the path of love.

14

Rate-Me-Rank-Me

When You Compare, You Disappear

P eter Oswald was cool. I met him when we were both six and a half, on the first day of elementary school, and we stayed together for the next six years. He wasn't one of my true muckers, like Stevie, Miles, Mike, and Tim were. He didn't come by my house for mammoth *Space Invader* sessions, didn't play on sports teams with us. And yet I always honored him with a deep respect. I might even have been a little intimidated by him.

It was his little acts of rebellion that first drew me to him. While I was busy trying to make myself invisible at school, he would deliberately commit small infractions to wind up the prefects. His favorite microrebellion was to stand with a microbend in his legs at assembly. We were all supposed to stand at attention, legs straight, back straight, arms behind the back. Peter's back would be ramrod straight, his arms perfectly clasped behind him, but his knees would display this small but perceptible kink in them. Each morning the prefects would walk the rows, stop at Peter, and ask him to straighten his knees. Whereupon he would straighten them ever so slightly, but not completely. The prefects would ask him again. An infinitesimal straightening from Peter.

He said nothing during these encounters. Just stared dead ahead, and almost but not quite obeyed their instructions. Even when one prefect called the others over to assess the relative straightness of Peter's legs, still he said nothing. A group of thirteen-year-old giants staring down at this little boy, sure that they were being played, but not sure how to define his crime or what to do about it.

He was over in team Sarnsfield, so I could never hear what they were all saying, but I could see the tableau of mini-oppression and resistance, and I was in awe. While I was shuddering at the thought that any prefect would even notice my existence, Peter was deliberately drawing their attention and ire. He was making himself a target, and showing the rest of us what was possible.

He was Steve McQueen in *The Great Escape*. Simply the coolest. (Go watch it.)

When we were eleven, I found myself in the same English class as Peter. We were just beginning to be introduced to the idea that studying English required not only reading, but also writing. Actual essays. Composition, words and phrases, structure, all of our own making. We were unwilling students of this new skill. With each new writing assignment, we'd whine, "How long does it have to be? Is this a one-paragraph paper, or a three-para?" (Or, god forbid, a fiver?) We thought of writing like a cross-country run in drizzle: the shorter the better.

Except Peter. I found him one afternoon scribbling away at his desk.

"What are you doing?" I asked him.

"Writing."

"What are you writing? Do we have an essay due?"

"Don't know. I'm not writing an essay. I'm writing a story."

"What sort of story?"

"A war story."

"Soldiers and tanks and guns and bullets? That kind of story?"

"Yes."

"How long is it?"

"Seventeen pages."

Seventeen pages! I thought. *Whoa! No one writes anything more than five paragraphs! What's with seventeen pages?* He was writing in blue ballpoint pen on regular lined paper. He was halfway down his current sheet, and underneath I could see a stack of pages all covered with his blue, rounded handwriting.

"Can I read it?" I asked.

He kept the sheet he was writing on and handed over the other pages. I started reading. And couldn't stop. This eleven-year-old kid had created a cast of characters—I could see them all, hear their voices, feel their fear—and then put them into scenarios and challenges that I could visualize so clearly. Those seventeen pages sucked me right in.

"Wow," I said. "What's going to happen next? Are you going to keep writing? How's it going to end? Do they all die?"

"Come back tomorrow," he said.

I went home that night transformed. Writing was not something to be avoided. Writing was cool. Writing could be filled with character and story and was exciting and scary and could go on and on and on for seventeen pages. Or more.

If cool-man Peter could do that, then why not me? It didn't look that hard. He wasn't studying. He was just sitting there at his desk with his pen and his paper and pulling all these people and scenes and words right out of his head.

I sat down to write. Page after page flowed out of me. Lots and lots of words, actual writing that filled up so much space. My mom came in and asked me what I was doing. "Writing," I replied. She smiled. I glowed. Turned back to my paper, wrote more words, and filled up more pages than I'd ever filled up before. Getting tired, I signed off my last page with " . . . to be continued," like I'd seen Peter do, and went to bed.

The next day I woke early and cycled off to school so that, before the assembly bell, I could read everything I'd written the night before.

I tried to lose myself in the story. Tried to be impressed. But I couldn't even begin to convince myself that I'd written an actual story. In the cold light of day I simply didn't believe anything I'd written. The characters seemed fake—I mean, of course they seemed fake; I'd just made them up. The challenges I'd placed them in were boring, or obvious, or anyway not real, since I'd just made them up as well. I managed to get through all eight pages, but when I was done I felt no desire to read on. Didn't want to ask the author what was going to happen next. Didn't care.

I was so sad and disappointed. And confused. Peter had done it. Why couldn't I? What did he know that I didn't? I went off to ask him.

"I don't know," he replied. "I just see these characters in my head and know how they should be with each other. Then I write it down. Why don't you keep at it? I'll read your stuff if you like."

I did keep at it, I think because filling up the pages gave me a feeling of power and accomplishment. But the stories never got any better. They remained—to my mind and, though he was sweet about it, to Peter's—boring and fake. The words did not transport you into another world. Instead, they were heavy and clumsy, something the reader had to wade through to get to the end.

Even at that young age I knew I would never be able to do what Peter could. If this was what writers did, then I wasn't one. I gave up writing for pleasure, and for the next twenty years carried around with me the caricature of myself that I was no writer because I was no Peter. This caricature was so pronounced that when I received a book contract to write my first book, the clause I was most concerned with was about money for a ghostwriter in the likely event that I couldn't deliver a book worth reading.

What I should have realized is that though I am no Peter, it doesn't mean I am no writer. It turns out that I am neither interested in making, nor very good at making, fiction. I find no characters popping into my head, and when I try to fabricate them, I get bored of them before I can even begin to describe them on paper. Fictional worlds and people are created by artists who believe passionately in the need for these worlds and people to come into existence. While I can appreciate such artists, I am not one of them.

Peter, God bless him, was a compelling exemplar of Peter. He was a rotten exemplar of me. By not realizing this, by confusing admiration with association, by aspiring to become him, I took myself down singularly unhappy and unproductive paths. I should have stayed on my true path.

(By the way, in preparation for writing this book, since we'd long ago lost touch, I looked up Peter Oswald. It turns out that he became a poet and a playwright. He was the first artist in residence at Shakespeare's Globe Theatre in London. Although he has created many lauded pieces, he is best known for his war plays.)

To help you see yourself for the unique creature you are, begin by resisting the pull of comparison. This is easy to write, and so very hard to do. Our entire systems of parenting, of schooling, of social media, and of working have been designed to force you to compare all aspects of you with your peers.

Your parents were given charts to compare your height, weight, crawling, pooping, walking, eating, sleeping, socializing, first word, first sentence against standardized norms. From the moment you are conceived to the moment you become an adult, your parents are primed to measure their own success by which percentile you fall into.

Your school doubles down on this fetish for comparison. The grades you're given throughout your education are derived by comparing your work against school, state, or national norms, and then pinpointing where you fall in this normative distribution. These norms locate you and define you. And, of course, determine which opportunities will be given to you, and which will not.

At work, this comparison fetish becomes an obsession. How much money you earn, whether you will get promoted, whether you will get laid off, all of these will be determined by your performance rating. And this rating is determined by your organization comparing you against everyone else. If you are perceived to be better than everyone else, you will be given a 5. If you're more middle-of-the-pack, you'll get a 3.

Some organizations derive these ratings by comparing each person's performance and potential. Some go further and define lists of skills that each person is supposed to possess—these are called *competencies*—and then rate you on how much of each skill you appear to possess, as compared with your peers.

Some, fearing that too many workers will be given high ratings, demand that only a certain percentage be given 5s and 4s, and that the rest receive 3s or lower. This is called *forcing the curve*. It means that, even if you compare favorably with your peers, you may still wind up with a low rating.

These systems of comparison serve the organization—grades help schools determine their ranking, and therefore their funding; ratings help companies hand out different levels of merit and bonus pay.

None of them serve you. Instead, by comparing you with others, they render you invisible. They use standardized criteria as the measure of you. Which is how they hide you. From yourself, and from everyone else.

Just Heavenly

Of course, there are times when the pressure to compare comes not from you, nor from your parents or boss, but instead from your friends. From folks who look at you, compare their life choices with yours, and, because they feel the comparison doesn't portray them favorably, denigrate you and your journey. These kinds of comparisons are the worst. They cut through your defenses the fastest, and are then the hardest to shake. The judgy judgments of "allies."

Here's an example from Myshel's journal, as she tries to make sense of her friends' reaction to her juggling of work and family.

_____

We rented a house in Heavenly, Lake Tahoe. Four fun families meant eight adults and ten kids. I didn't pack ski snacks or wool thermals. My two boys' wrists were exposed, revealing their jackets belonged to last season. I was the working mom.

I drove up stressed. Don't get me wrong. Watching the boys shred down the mountain, with the bigness of their smiles competing with the bigness of the mountain, made me happy. But I couldn't turn off work. Not only was I the only executive on staff that had committed to a winter vacation with the family, but I was the only executive that would be on vacation while we ruined 30 percent of our staff's lives by laying them off.

Yep. It was that week.

Après-ski. We shuffle through the cold and into the warm cabin. Brian lights the fire, grabs his computer, and announces to the crew that he has to get some work in. It's Tuesday. All the moms nod with appreciation for Brian. He is the emperor penguin, taking care of his family. He will starve and work while his wife replenishes herself after a long ski day. He'll eat later. We wave him away, beaming with pride. Heather tosses powdered sugar on him like confetti.

Tess, Brian's wife, begins baking the homemade ziti pasta dish she'd carefully prepared ahead of the trip. Jill is putting blue sprinkles on her homemade cupcakes, then runs to her bag, forgetting she'd bought pink sprinkles for Ava, the only girl in the lot. The kids screech with delight, seeing the sky-high mounds of white frosting atop a rich chocolate cake. "It looks like snow!" they say.

I make myself a Moscow mule.

"We are meeting in twenty minutes. Does that work for you?" My colleagues know I'm on vacation, but the text comes anyway. At 8:30 p.m. "Yes, of course," I text back, knowing it will be absolute hell to extract myself from the Trivial Pursuit (drinking-game version) circle.

All the kids are in the upstairs loft, watching the cult ski film *Aspen Extreme*. Jill puts Ava in charge of the bell. When a kissing scene happens, she rings and Jill runs up to cover little Mikey's eyes. I was waiting for the bell. The first kiss.

The bell rings, Jill jumps up, I jump with her and slip out and into the bedroom to take the call. Only four people are on the line. *Oh good, I'm not late*, I think. We're waiting for our CEO. Oh, no, we aren't. The board wants to include the CEO in the layoffs. They want to do it tomorrow. I will have to fire our CEO tomorrow from the Heavenly ski lounge. In pink pants and fleece. I start yanking on my hair. Nobody can see. I am in a room walled with flannel. They start asking me legal questions.

"DRRIIINNKK! You need to drink!" forty-year-old adults yell in the background. I catapult myself into the small walk-in closet, cold hands fumbling at the mute button. "Hello? Are you there?" my colleagues ask. I wait for the cabin roar to cease. "Yep, sorry, I was on mute. Yes, we'll have to put a solid severance package together."

I talk as though I am sitting upright in a glistening glass office with a pantsuit on. Instead of soggy socks and my nine-year-old son's sweats. I forgot to pack loungewear.

Forty-five minutes later, the call ends and Mighty Moms are still gaming loudly, keeping up with the dad pack. I wait for the kissing bell so I can slither back in. My beanie's too bright, I'm caught.

"Seriously? It's ten o'clock at night and you're working on vacation." Eyeroll, headshake; stare. I disappoint them.

The next day I fire our CEO from the ski lounge.

That night I game with the crew.

When my phone buzzes, Mighty Moms throw up their hands as if they're stopping cars for their kids to use the school crosswalk. "Nope! Not tonight! It's called vacation! It's called boundaries! It's ridiculous that they think you'll take a meeting on vacation. Is it worth it? There's no way I'd ever miss a Little League game. I literally wouldn't be able to live with myself. I don't know how you do it."

Brian, the working dad, has missed Little League games.

Brian worked every single day on that vacation.

Brian was celebrated.

I earn more money than most of the men in that musty cabin. I work hard to take care of my family. Why don't I get showered with sugar confetti?

Why aren't I an emperor penguin?

———————————

Clearly, this is a specific form of comparison: one woman being pressured by other women who are comparing their life choices with hers, and judging her in the process.

Brian found love in his job. So did she. Brian got to play these loves out without having to fight against the "joking" condemnation of others. Instead, they would ask him about his work, what he was excited about, what his goals were, and he got to describe and revel in his loves. His audience affirmed and amplified his loves. He got bigger in their eyes.

Whatever the opposite of support is, that's what Myshel got. And not from enemies, from folks trying to do her wrong, but from her closest confidantes. And so she, like so many women in the workplace, didn't get to amplify her loves. She got to apologize for them instead.

Obviously, I don't have a solution to all of the comparisons that'll force themselves into your field of vision and distort how you come to see yourself. What I can offer you is this:

First, no matter how penetrating the stares or how caustic the judgments of others, *hold on tight to your own red threads*. They are yours. Other people may tell you who they think you should be, but you know, better than anyone, what your loves are and how they make you feel. There is truth and power in these red threads. Weave them ever more tightly into the fabric of your life, show others how you are using them to make a contribution, and over time you may find that the fabric you've woven is strong enough both to hold you and to block them out.

Second, *be careful whom you choose to surround yourself with*. Take seriously the truth that those closest to you do indeed reach in and touch you. It's inhuman to pretend that they don't. Do the people closest to you truly want you to flourish? Do they genuinely want to support you in turning all you love into all you could contribute? If they don't, then you do not have a good relationship with them. And sometimes the best way to fix a bad relationship is to get out of it.

Third, if you feel a need to compare yourself with others, *keep your eyes focused always and only on contribution*. On the outcome of your efforts. Never compare your methods with theirs. If you are working with a colleague who seems able to turn customers' frustration around, then yes, admire this outcome. If a teammate excels at crafting presentations that get her the funding she seeks, then yes, acknowledge the value of this outcome—and even, if you so desire, aspire to it.

But try to resist the temptation to copy or compare yourself with others' methods. Their way is not your way, and never will be. Other people's methods are a mystery to you, as yours are to them.

The best way forward for you is to admire the contribution of others and then figure out your most instinctive and authentic way of achieving that same outcome. Don't compare your way of selling, serving, writing, presenting, or leading with others', because you will lose yourself in the comparison. Instead, seek your path of least resistance to that same outcome.

What is a Pollock to a Matisse to an O'Keefe, or a Chris Rock to a Jerry Seinfeld to an Amy Schumer, or a Cardi B to a Beyoncé to an Ed Sheeran, or a Nelson Mandela to a Barack Obama to a Malala Yousafzai? Each represents a different route on a similar journey. So, yes, admire the painter for how they open up your world. Admire the comedian for how they make you laugh. Admire the singer for how they move you. Admire the Nobel Peace Prize winner for their impact on the world. But to compare how they did it, and to expect that each mimic the others—well, it's a fool's game, isn't it.

Finally, *remember the massive extent of your uniqueness.* Five thousand Milky Ways. No one compares with you, and no one ever will. Your pattern of connections, insights, instincts, loves, and loathes is unmatched and unmatchable.

This doesn't make you better than anyone else. It just makes any comparison of you with anyone else a failure of imagination.

15

Suckitup

Love Is Not a Luxury

The scariest devil on your whole journey may be the last: Suckitup.

He will tell you that your entire quest is a waste of time. That most jobs just suck, are to be endured not enjoyed, and that what you need to do is take a deep breath when you go to work, do your job, and then come home. Reserve love for your friends and family.

I first came upon this devil during my research into the talents of the world's best housekeepers.

"What is it with you and housekeepers?" a Wharton professor asked me back then. "Apparently, they fascinate you."

Apparently, they do. I featured a team of Walt Disney World housekeepers in my first book, *First, Break All the Rules*, and a different group from Hilton in the follow-up, *Go Put Your Strengths to Work*.

I think the reason I'm so intrigued by them is that theirs is one of those jobs that we condescend to. *Anyone can do that job,* we think to ourselves, and if we were unlucky enough to have to do it, we would count the days until we could get ourselves promoted out of it. And yet here I was interviewing the ten best housekeepers at Walt Disney World, and to hear them tell it, it was interesting, challenging work that they loved.

"What do you love about it?" I asked them. A whole range of different answers:

> "I love vacuuming myself backward out of each room. Taking the mess of a room and turning it into perfectly straight vacuum lines. Love that!"

> "Busy check-out days. There's so much to do, getting the carts filled up just right, everyone moving so fast."

> "Making a show for our guests. I'll arrange the fluffy toys in a little scene so that one day the kids'll come back and find Mickey and Minnie dancing on the windowsill, and the next day I'll put Donald and Goofy with one arm around each other and the other on the remote control or an empty French fry container, so the kids think that while they were out at the park, Donald and Goofy hung out snacking and watching TV."

English, Portuguese, Haitian Creole, Spanish, a chorus of housekeepers who were all excellent at their job, none of whom knew each other, and who all found things to love in housekeeping. To hear them tell it, not only was this a hard job to excel at, but if you did excel, it was the kind of work that they would *not* want to get themselves promoted out of. A number of them had been offered the chance to move into a supervisory role and had turned it down.

These outstanding housekeepers gave the lie to the view that finding love in your work is a luxury, one most of us can't afford. The view that work is called "work" for a reason. That you should not define yourself or try to find yourself through your work. That you are not your work. That you go to work to earn money—that's it—and you return with this money and then use it to provide for those you love. Just suck it up.

Toni Morrison once quoted her dad sharing this view with her after she complained to him about her work: "Listen, you don't live there. You live here. With your people. Go to work. Get your money. And come on home."

Barbara Ehrenreich, in her book *Nickel and Dimed: On (Not) Getting By in America*, played out this same view in greater depth. Basically, she spent a year getting herself hired for what she considered menial labor, and then wrote a book about how awful and soul-destroying these jobs were. And about how, if we were going to coerce people to do house-cleaning or manufacturing jobs, then we should pay them a heck of a lot more to suffer through this loveless work.

This isn't the place to get into a debate about wages—though, frankly, I agree with her that the wage disparity between frontline workers and senior leadership has reached an obscene level. But what we can say is that virtually any job is awful and soul-destroying if it is being done by a person who doesn't find love in it.

Listening to those housekeepers describe their work, they made it sound exciting and intriguing and chock full of variety. Whereas Barbara's description of the very same job sounded horrific.

Here's another horrific-sounding job: doing research for a year, organizing the interviews, keeping copious notes, arranging those notes, and then figuring out how to turn them into a compelling book. That's Barbara's job, and to millions of people it sounds utterly soul-destroying. But not to Barbara. She loves it.

Same with the housekeeping job. Sounds soul-destroying to Barbara, but not to the hundreds of amazing housekeepers I've interviewed. They love it.

Who's right? Well, no one is. Or rather, they all are. Each of us finds love in different activities, people, situations, and outcomes. We all need to be very careful that we don't impose our loves on other people and assume that, just because we love putting words on a page but hate cleaning a bathroom, everyone shares these feelings. Just because you hate a certain job doesn't make it hateful to everyone.

Or, turning that around, we shouldn't assume anyone performing a job excellently must find love in all aspects of it. As the Mayo Clinic research from chapter 6 suggests, the goal should be to find love in at least 20 percent of it. And in any job, if you find that you don't love 20 percent of it, if the percentage slips to 15 percent, 10 percent, or, God forbid, zero, then you are far more likely to experience burnout, accidents on the job, and to start medicating yourself with absences, alcohol, and drugs.

In any job, sustained excellence without love is impossible. Love isn't a luxury. It's a necessity.

Of course, there will be occasions—many, many occasions—when companies create loveless jobs, and when supervisors take zero interest in which aspects of your work you love and how you can turn this into contribution.

If, for example, a company creates warehouse roles with little space for exercising judgment or even taking bathroom breaks, then no matter how many mental games the workers play to try to get through the day, they will always be just getting through the day, enduring the work rather than contributing what they love.

Or if teachers are given so few financial resources they can't even buy supplies for their class, and so many students they can't pay attention to each one, it's hard to see how they could find love in this overstretched, underfunded world.

Indeed, one of the goals of this book is to get companies and managers to realize the benefits—in the form of fewer lost workdays, higher-quality work, less burnout, better student outcomes—of designing a role around what the best people in that role love about it. Use love as the design criteria for a job—any job—and it will look very different from the inhuman job descriptions and mandates so many have to suffer through.

Back when I was interviewing those Walt Disney World housekeepers, the irony wasn't lost on me that, though the best ones lay on the bed and turned on the ceiling fan because this is the first thing a guest does after a long day at the park, their formal job description actually forbade them from lying on the bed. And those housekeepers who arranged the kids' toys in a different little scene each day? They were breaking the regulation to not touch more of the guest's possessions than is necessary to clean the room.

Design a job as though there's no love in it, and it's a self-fulfilling prophecy—you wind up designing loveless jobs in which the best have to actually break the rules and regulations in order to find love in what they do. As far as we can, it's up to us to try to persuade our leaders that this is wrong. That if we can define jobs through the lens of those who love them then higher performance, higher quality, and less burnout are the happy result.

Love Lives in Motion, Not in Balance

Love isn't just a feeling. It is a source of energy, and like all energy sources, it must flow. For you, for me, for all of us, a healthy life isn't one where we find balance. A "balanced" life—where your work, your family, your finances, your dreams are all perfectly in sync—is not only nigh impossible to achieve, but even if you did achieve it, that life would be stationary and stagnant, with you tiptoeing along thinking, *Please, don't anyone move! I've got everything just so!*

Instead, a healthy life is one where you are in motion, where you are moving through life—all aspects of your life—in such a way that you draw strength and love from it, and this then gives you the energy you need to keep moving.

This means to live happily and fully, you have to express your loves. Yes, they spring from within you, but then they demand expression. You've got to get them out somewhere, somehow, turn them from loves into actions, from passions into contributions. And when you do, your life feels coherent and authentic, and you know, you just know, in every fiber of your being, that you are on your path.

The inverse is also true, though. If you love doing something, anything—organizing, writing, designing, challenging, teaching—and you are prevented from doing it, then your life starts to feel wrong. It might feel to you like frustration. It might feel like anger, or depression, or confusion. You sitting on the couch crying to yourself and not knowing why. You finding yourself short-tempered and impatient, pushing away those who want to help you. You walking around in a brain fog, wondering where all the creativity and quick-wittedness went.

In your quiet moments you ask yourself, *Where did I go? What's wrong with me? I don't think I recognize me anymore. I don't think I like me anymore.*

It's the oddest feeling, isn't it. Love seems like such a positive emotion—it opens you up, bringing you new ideas, a generous spirit, a collaborative heart—and yet, love unexpressed transforms into a caustic, abrasive thing, withering you from the inside. Your loves—the very things that can elevate and reveal the very best of you—can, when bottled up, burn away any signs of who you really are and turn you into a husk of a person.

My mom, Jo—who loves reading about the origins of the world's great religions—found this verse in the Gospel of Thomas. It captures perfectly the dangers of loves repressed: "If you bring forth what is within you, what you bring forth will save you. If you do not bring forth what is within you, what you do not bring forth will destroy you."

So, no, Suckitup, loves are not a luxury, reserved for the precious few. Loves, expressed, are a necessity for us all. Stifle them, deny them, block their flow, and they will destroy you from the inside out.

But identify them, honor them, and let them flow into contribution, and you will become the biggest and most powerful version of you.

Part Three

Make Love +
Work Come Alive

So now we get into the nitty-gritty. Precisely how you can follow what you love to a life that feels fully your own. Love sounds so lovely, but it also sounds soft, squishy, idealistic even. How can you create for yourself a more loving way of living when you're faced every day with a world so busy it doesn't even see you?

In this part of the book I'm going to try to be as practical as possible for you. We're going to start with your relationships since no matter where you are on your journey, you'll need to rely on others to help you. Then we'll dive into your career—what can you do to find paths that truly fit you, in the face of so much workplace change? Then leading—specifically, how can you lead teams so that you give each team member the greatest possible chance to contribute what they love to the organization's mission? And more broadly, which practices and characteristics reveal that your organization takes each person's loves seriously? What does a true Love + Work organization look like?

Finally, we'll look at how love can help you and others learn. Your school, college, and workplace training are all built without much focus on what you love. How can we all come together to remake learning so that it honors the uniqueness already there inside of you.

There's quite a lot of prescription and action in this part of the book, so hang on to your hat, pick up your red pen, and let's get cracking: What can you actually do to make love and work come alive?

16

I See You, I Love You

Your Love + Work Relationship

Should I leave?

It's the summer of 2015, and these days I cannot get this question out of my head. It stays with me all day long. I go to bed with it. It jolts me awake me in the long, slow hours of the night. In the morning I bring it with me on my jog, at work, in the car, driving too fast, place to place, trying to turn up the wind noise and drown out the question. *Should I leave?*

I am not a leaver. I know that much. I know I've always been in love with love. My favorite movies growing up were *Doctor Zhivago, Charade, Heaven Can Wait, The Last of the Mohicans*, those movies where the audience is rooting for two people to find each other and hold on forever, no matter what occurs. I'm a lover of lovers. One-on-one true intimacy. Soul mates. That's the sexiest.

In 2015 I've been married for almost twenty years. We have two beautiful kids, the house, the dogs, the friends, some measure of financial stability—go down the checklist, and it's a really good life. And I have no one else pulling me out of this life. No siren song of a new relationship tempting me away.

So what's wrong with me? Why does this question ring in my head like a medieval church bell calling me to account? To kneel. To listen to myself. To hear the questions: *Should I leave? What the hell is wrong with me? How can I even contemplate putting my family through this?*

And yet I can. I am. Contemplating it. Obsessed by it. It consumes me.

To the outside observer all seems well—my smile is still affixed—but inside I can't feel myself. The only thing I look forward to in my day is the shower—the water pounding on my head drowns out the questions. But then I dry off, and the day's activities tumble down upon me, and as I fight them off, deflect them, barrel through them, I find no joy in what I'm doing. I am going through the motions of life, letting nothing in. I'm a shield, protecting an emptiness.

In 2015 I woke up every day lost.

And then, well, then quite a lot happened.

In 2016 I did leave my marriage of twenty years.

In 2017 the company I'd spent a decade building was sold.

In 2018 my ex was embroiled in a national scandal.

In 2020 the pandemic hit and changed all our lives in ways we're all still discovering.

I left the family house on February 15, 2016, climbed into the car, drove over to a friend's house, crying and giddy and certain and clueless. My worst day as a husband and as a father. I knew so little, knew only that I was vanishing and that this wouldn't end well for any of us if I stayed.

I'm still trying to make my peace with what I did. If you've been through divorce, you'll know what I mean. It is an overwhelming experience, and takes years before you gain any sort of perspective. Please don't listen to anyone telling you how to get through a divorce until they are at least three years into it. Things change. Wisdom comes slowly. I can't even scratch the surface of the emotions I've felt—so much guilt wrapped in shame, some happiness, so much pain. All I can say now is that though I am proud of my life choices, I will never be proud to be divorced. I know it was the right decision, and, still, it will always feel like a failure.

Like everyone who's been through it, I was a mess that first year after leaving. I've never been bipolar, but that year I exhibited all the symptoms. Each manic, action-packed day would be followed by a dark day. I'd spent my marriage closing myself off and filling the hours with events and transactions, and now, alone, the silence was loud and dark. One weekend, disgusted with myself for spending so many hours alone on my bed, weeping into the pillow, I adopted a rescue dog, Fitzy, to keep me company. The next weekend found me spending the same hours with him on the same bed, this time weeping into his fur—a bitey, squirmy, scruffy-brown pillow.

On some level I knew I was desperate for connection; but I wouldn't have been able to articulate this need to you. I felt jagged, a danger to myself and others. My one mental refrain was that I wanted to be alone. This way I wouldn't hurt anyone.

I Am Because You Are

I had known Myshel for ages, had worked with her for ages, and hadn't thought much about her beyond her role at work. I'm boring that way. Work hard, go home.

Then she started in with her questions.

"What do you mean by reliable data?"

Or, "Why do you say that frequency trumps quality? I have no idea what that means."

Or, "How do you know someone's personality doesn't change much during the course of their life?"

We were shooting a series of videos and, unused as I was to anyone engaging with me in this kind of genuine way, I thought she was playacting the interviewer for the camera. But no, she was just curious. Unrelentingly curious. And each time my broken-glass state of mind made me defensive about her questions, she'd laugh and say, "No, really, I genuinely can't get my mind around that. I love the concept, but play it out for me."

And I'd play it out. And she'd ask some more. And whatever defensiveness I might have felt twinges of waned as I followed her questions down to the core concept underpinning this or that idea. Which for me is the beautiful, glorious point of it all, one of my red threads. Which she seemed to know.

Then she'd name my negative patterns in some way that called them out, but also somehow wove them into something positive—or rather, something that stood a chance of being woven into something positive.

I can sometimes say no to things too quickly—my instinct is to reject an idea if all my mental drawers are still filled up with existing ideas. I know this isn't necessarily an admirable quality, that it can be bloody annoying to others. In her words, though, it became "Immediate Rejection Syndrome"—which she found funny. And a sign not of pathology and weakness, but of my need to not engage with a new idea before I'd truly come to the end of the one I happened to be chewing on.

This was good. A strength, even, that could be channeled intelligently.

The naming of Immediate Rejection Syndrome was the product of someone seeing a quirk, recognizing it as a pattern, and delighting in it. She wasn't patting me on the head for it—it's a quirk, after all, and quirks can grate. She was just recognizing something specific in me and then expecting me to figure out how it could be used to make a contribution.

Intimacy, in my experience, had been for generating evidence to be used against me. But intimacy for generating understanding, and for sharing that understanding lovingly? No, I wasn't used to this. I was suspicious of it. It took me a long while to remember that intimacy can lift you up.

Think back on what Dr. Don Clifton did. He saw and trusted in my loves. He didn't tell me to wait. He let these loves of mine run. He knew that they were more powerful than any formal program that Gallup had put together. Not that he didn't expect me to learn and build my expertise. He did. But he knew that my loves would be the best impetus and integrating point for my learning. Since I would learn more and faster through my loves, he would go with them and push to one side that I was "too young" or "not ready." Love would make me ready.

Do you have people in your life who are this trusting of what you love?

I ask because one of the most important lessons to learn on your journey is that you are not alone. You are often told that you should not pay attention to what others think, that other people's opinions of you are none of your business. And yet we are social creatures, each of us equipped with those mirror neurons to ensure that when you feel pain, I feel it too. When you laugh, I laugh with you. We are all of us acutely sensitive to the reactions we see and feel in those around us. This isn't a problem to be fixed, or a pathology to be cured of. It is our very essence. Each of us is the catalyst to those around us. Each of us is the power source to those we love and lead. Put more simply, you will flourish only in response to another human being.

So, the question for you is: Which human beings have you surrounded yourself with, and which parts of you do they see?

A very few of us might be clear-eyed enough to find ourselves all by ourselves. The rest of us need help. Our noses are pressed up so closely to our own selves that we can no longer see what makes us beautiful and powerful. We need another human being to draw back the cloak of measurement and judgment, and reveal—to us and to everyone else—what's been hidden.

You won't be taught this. Our lessons are founded on the ideas of ancient Greek thinkers—Plato and Aristotle, primarily—who didn't place much value on how much we need one another. They tell us that virtuous behavior comes from having a virtuous character. That each of us should aspire to develop such a character. That we are our own moral universe and that, independent of anyone else, we should be able to withstand our unhealthy impulses, conquer weakness, and make wise choices about our actions. That to live the best version of yourself, you must deliberately build within you the attributes required for such perfection.

No knock on Plato, or you, Aristotle, but I know I'm not that perfect a person. It sure sounds uplifting for someone to tell me that all the resources I will ever need can be found within me, but my day-to-day reality doesn't feel like that. Instead, it feels like I am bumping into my imperfections all the time.

I know I am too quick to judge an idea or a course of action; I know I interrupt folks on my team too quickly and that they can start to feel unheard; I know I rebel instinctively against the predictability of project plans, and instead happily dive down a rabbit hole just because I think it might lead somewhere intriguing. Which it might, but seeing the frustration of the rest of my team, I know my rabbit-hole diving can be a selfish indulgence.

I know I hate mingling.

I know I hate discipline and routine, the very routine that might help others feel organized and in control.

I know how defensive I can get, and that, when challenged, I can become louder, not wiser.

I know this is wrong. I know all of these are anti-attributes, things to be fixed, bad behavior. If I was following the Platonic ideal, I would spend my life working to embrace these flaws of mine, labeling them "areas of opportunity," figuring out how to withstand their inherent temptations and instead cultivate new, much more admirable attributes within me.

But I find I can't do that. God knows I've tried. Why do I hate mingling? I'm good at it, so I should love it. And yet I hate the stress of having to strike up a conversation, sink into it just enough to make the person feel appreciated—but not so much that I can't, at just the right moment, wind up our little chat so I can break away, sidle up to the next person, and start up a slightly different but substantially similar conversation. And all the while there's pressure to remember each person's name and something distinct about them, or their work, or their new cat, or their new car, or something. The stress of all that. It never leaves me.

And routines. Why do I rebel against them like a child? Why do I not look at my calendar the night before? Why do I deliberately call in late to our standing Tuesday morning team meeting? Why do I get a slight kick out of not meeting a deadline that some well-intended teammate has imposed on us?

I can see myself doing these things. I can see how counterproductive they are. And yet still I do them. Why?

Have you had a similar realization? That you have certain predictable patterns within you, and that some of these patterns don't serve you one bit. And that the backbeat to your life is a thrumming reminder that you can fix this if you just worked at it, that you are the source of your own virtue, that you contain all you could ever need to examine and perfect your imperfections. It won't be Plato's voice telling you this— it might be your mom's, your high school math teacher's, or your boss's—but whoever is saying it, it's loud and persuasive. The voice tells you about original sin, and self-help, and the growth mindset, and how ten thousand hours of deliberate practice can transform you into whatever you set your mind to be. That you can perfect yourself, and you alone are the one to do it.

There's a wealth of recent data revealing how wrong-headed this all is—from brain science to rigorous studies of high performers—but the Aztecs knew centuries ago how enduringly unique we all are, and therefore how much we need one another. Their concept of virtue and goodness was not centered on the individual. Instead, it was relational, as in no person is perfect and so none of us should strive to be. In their telling, virtue—and contribution, and creativity, and resilience, and altruism, and all things good—come about only when two people connect with each other.

When one person sees the failings in another, they step in to help. I don't like parties, so the other person doesn't make me go to parties; or does, but then stands by me so that I don't have to mingle; or wanders by me every few minutes and rescues me from each too deep/too shallow conversation.

When one person sees the behavior patterns in another, they guide them toward the most positive expression of those patterns. I don't like structure, so the other person shows me how to channel my instinctive improvisation toward creating something new and valuable.

When one person sees the trap the other is about to fall into, they nudge him around it. If I'm about to react defensively, the other person finds just the right way to remind me that, if I'm so enamored of my concepts, I should be able to withstand, even welcome, any new ideas or evidence.

Now that I'm writing this, I realize how close the Aztec view was to Archbishop Desmond Tutu's Ubuntu philosophy: "A person is a person only through other persons."

That's not the very rational idea of "I think, therefore I am."

But instead: "I am because you are."

We exist and are uplifted only through our connection to another person. We will be good, and noble, and our biggest and most powerful versions of ourselves only through the eyes and heart of another.

How to See with Love

On my life's journey I've lived this out in a pragmatic way— I've built teams of people whose strengths complemented mine, and an entire company of people who were dedicated to helping our clients build these same sort of diverse teams.

What I missed, and what got me so lost in my personal life, was the emotional power of being seen for who I truly am.

Love, in any relationship, is not protection—it is not someone reaching in and saving you from yourself.

Love is not diversity—it is not someone complementing your personality with different strengths.

Love is not similarity—it is not someone sharing your interests, or values, or dreams.

Love is someone seeing the fullness of you and wanting you to be the best possible version of you. This is what a relationship is for—any relationship, whether friend, business partner, sibling, or lover. It is for each person to do all they can to help the other express their uniqueness as powerfully as possible. Love's goal is to make the other person bigger.

You do not need the other person to love what you love. You need only for them to love that you love what you love, and to want to help you turn your loves into contribution. All of this starts with them seeing you. Because they cannot love what they cannot see.

The research on love in relationships reveals quite a lot about what it means to "see with love."

Firstly, and weirdly, it doesn't appear to mean seeing your partner with dispassionate accuracy. In a series of longitudinal studies, researchers asked couples to rate one another on qualities such as "empathetic," "warm," and "decisive." The researchers' thesis was that the happiest couples would be the

ones whose ratings matched most closely—as in, if one partner rated the other high on "decisive" and lower on "warm,"
and the other partner rated themselves the same way, then
they'd be happier. Each would see in the other what they saw
in themselves.

But this is not at all what the researchers found. The data
showed that in the happiest couples, the partners each rated
the other high on *every single quality*. Which you might think
was merely a function of being in the throes of love on this
particular day. But then the researchers tracked these couples
over time and saw that the couples who rated each other high
on every single quality remained happier across time.

Seeing someone with love means keeping your rose-tinted
glasses on. The researchers called this your *benevolent dis-
tortion*. Thus your partner isn't disorganized, they're spontaneous. Not willful, but self-assured. Not flirtatious, but
charming. If you see your partner through the lens of benevolent distortions, then you become more confident in your decision to tie your life to your partner's. This confidence breeds
intimacy, and this intimacy strengthens your love, which
leads to yet more benevolent distortions, and so to more confidence, to more intimacy, in an ongoing upward spiral of love.

Another aspect of seeing with love relates not just to your
partner's attributes, but also to their motives. In the best relationships, the researchers found, each partner always looked
for the most generous explanation for the other's behavior.
And once they landed on it, they believed it.

The belief in the most generous explanation served the relationship. It fostered confidence in each partner, this confidence bred intimacy, this intimacy fueled love.

That finding is yet one more piece of evidence for why we need to tread carefully around feedback. The data reveals that the very best relationships are not those where one partner is digging like a detective for the "real" reasons the other partner did something, and then confronting them with the hard truth of this reality. Instead, the best relationships are built when both partners feel like the other will believe the best possible reasons for their behavior.

This is not saying that seeing with love means giving your partner a pass, or an excuse, or an alibi—if your partner has let you down, it doesn't serve the relationship for you to stifle or censor your actual feelings. It means simply that the reasons any of us do anything are complex and opaque—even to ourselves. We thrive *only* in relationships where our partner admits this complexity, and always tacks toward the explanations that show us in the best possible light. Yes, this generosity serves us, but it also serves them—it boosts their confidence in us a little bit in this moment, and a lot over time.

When Myshel noticed my tendency to initially reject an idea, she could have chalked it up to me being intent on making sure only my own ideas held sway. Or to my unwillingness to let go of something I had long believed. Or even to me having a deep distrust of anything that I didn't come up with myself.

And goodness knows, maybe if I was on the therapist's couch, I would discover that, deep down, some of these un-flattering explanations did indeed animate me. I mean, I sure hope I'm not that person, but like all of us, I know that not all of my motives are free from amour propre, self-love.

Have you ever been in a relationship where your partner fancied themselves a therapist? Where they'd decided that their role was to reveal you to you, warts and all? It's exhaust-ing, isn't it? You have to spend your days on constant vigil, knowing that the person you are closest to is on the lookout for your darkest motives, and will, at some point soon, play these out for you in excruciating—and not wholly inaccurate—detail. You find yourself permanently on the defensive, always ready to step back, out of the spotlight, out of harm's way. And so you do, step back, and back, until one day you wake up and you've stepped so far back that you're psychologically separated from one another.

I find myself wrestling with how to write this, since, good grief, I don't want to hold my and Myshel's relation-ship up as an exemplar—we aren't an exemplar of anything except ourselves, with all the ups and downs this implies. But I do know how safe and lifted up I feel being in rela-tionship with someone who sees a quirk of mine, and rather than tearing the floorboards up to look for the "true cause" of my behavior, takes the sting out of it by giving it a silly nickname. With the quirk defanged, both of us can now not only laugh at it, but actually figure out how to use it to make me bigger.

Which leads to a final discovery from all this love research: when you see an imperfection in your partner, don't draw a line around it, label it a "weakness," and then try to balance it out with your partner's other good qualities. As in, "Yes, he's closed off to new ideas, but at least he's warm and creative." Or, "Yes, she's self-righteous, but at least she gets things done."

"Balancing" your partner's weaknesses and loves in this way might seem wise, but the data reveals that it doesn't work—partners who do this to one another end up with more doubts, more conflicts, and less rewarding relationships. By identifying your partner's weakness, you're giving it definition, and weight, and therefore power. When they're talking to you, they know that at any moment you might bring out their very clearly defined weakness and use it as a weapon against them.

The data recommends that when you see a failing in your partner, you should recast it in your mind as an aspect of something they love. Thus, for Myshel my Immediate Rejection Syndrome isn't defined in her mind as a weakness to be fixed. It's an aspect of me—loving the core concept of an idea so much that I can't entertain another idea until I've let go of the one I'm currently grinding on. She knows she can't rid me of Immediate Rejection Syndrome, because, if she did, then it would rip out all the stuff I so love about diving deep to the core of a concept. Diving deep in this way is my essence, my reddest of red threads, and the cause of much of whatever good I might do in the world. She knows this. And I know she knows this. And she knows I know she knows.

What a relief that is. What a lift. My loves come from the very heart of me. On occasion, yes, they lead to unproductive actions. For me, to be in a thriving relationship is to be seen by someone who is curious about my loves, who pays attention to what they create in me, and who's always trying to help me weave them into something fine and grand—even if, during one particular Sunday afternoon conversation, they might've woven something annoying.

So, on your life's journey, look to your left and to your right, and ask yourself whether you are choosing to travel with partners who are curious about you, who delight in your loves, and who want you to be the biggest version of you.

All you will be is because they are. Just as all they will be is because you are.

17

A Scavenger Hunt for Love

Your Love + Work Career

How do you feel your career is going right now?

You might be just starting out, in that glorious and also overwhelming frame of mind where the entire world lies open before you. Or you might be twenty years into your career and feeling fabulous about it. Or at a dead end, or like maybe you bet on entirely the wrong path. Or perhaps you're just marking time until your new side hustle blossoms into something that might actually pay the bills.

Wherever you are, how does it feel to you? Are you dragging? Are you super-excited? Are you a little bored? A little frightened? Or does it all just depend on the day, and your mood, or your boss's mood?

Your career is a cornerstone of your life. Sometimes you feel like you are standing so tall and straight upon it. And at other times you feel its weight on you, and you double over, legs buckling. It can be difficult to bear. You want to be financially successful, to support yourself, your family, pay your debts. And yet you don't want to sell out your soul. No matter what's in your bank account, you don't want to get to the end of your life and discover that you have been disconnected from your contribution to the world. Your job is one beautiful way—though far from the only one—in which you get to express the uniqueness inside of you. A series of jobs that cuts you off from yourself is a psychological mess, and, from all we're learning about the mind/body connection, a physiological mess as well.

Careers are tricky though, aren't they. We tend to think that the happy, healthy people are those who achieve a balance between work and life. And yet, as I touched on in chapter 15, balance is a false god. The healthy goal isn't to be balanced, not really. In nature everything healthy is moving, and thus a healthy life is one that enables you to move, and to draw enough strength from that movement to allow you to keep moving.

A healthy career is also in motion. It is a constant work in progress, always in a state of becoming. Just when you think you've found the perfect job, life moves on, and you find you need to start over—a new team, a new company, a new career. So, in the face of this perpetual motion machine, how can you apply the principles of Love + Work to your ever-changing, starting-over career?

I've spent most of my own career studying this question. Beginning with my master's thesis on the social and psychological issues of entrepreneurship, where we interviewed a hundred successful entrepreneurs and compared their choices with those of a hundred entrepreneurs whose businesses had failed. Then continuing with research projects at both Deloitte and Accenture, where we investigated how people had navigated their way up, around, and through these huge, labyrinthine organizations. And now on to our current Love + Work research project, where we are seeking to understand the nature of work through the lens of those who love it. My focus has always been: How do those who come to love their work as a full expression of themselves actually wind up in that sweet spot—and how do they keep moving that sweet spot right along with them?

Inevitably, I've looked at my own career to see what lessons, if any, can be drawn. After I graduated from university, why did I up and move from England to Lincoln, Nebraska? I could have gotten a job in London that would have kept me so much closer to home. Why the dramatic leap to a land I didn't know, to a company that would pay me half as much as my other offers, to a job that I hadn't studied for?

Why, ten years into my Nebraska sojourn, did I start to write? How hard-working, or skillful, or just plain lucky was I to emerge from my writing cave with books that people actually wanted to read? How the heck did that happen? Did

I know it would play out this way? If so, what was the secret sauce?

And then I left Gallup to start my own company. Did I know this would work out? Why did I give up a seventeen-year career and start over from scratch? Did I have a playbook I was running, or was I just making it up as I went along?

And then, a pivot. I had begun my company as a content and coaching firm, but somewhere along the way I decided that we needed to become a software company, powered by subscriptions. Did I know much about software? No, I knew very little. So why the pivot? And why was I so sure that this was right, even in the face of strong resistance from within my own team? And how the heck was I to know how to lead a team of a hundred engineers and product developers? Good grief. Be careful what you wish for.

When SurveyMonkey offered to buy 25 percent of the company, why did I so trust the CEO, Dave Goldberg, that I agreed? Why, when ADP came calling two years later and offered to buy the company outright, did I accept this offer when I had turned down so many others? And why, after the sale, was I so excited to continue my work through the ADP Research Institute? I didn't need to stay on, but there was no question in my mind that I would. And that I would do so with passion.

In all the standard ways of measuring such things, my career has worked out. Did I know what I was doing when I first jumped on that Greyhound bus from the airport to Lincoln, Nebraska, forty years ago?

Many of these questions I can't answer directly, other than to point to luck. Jim Collins, in his book *Good to Great*, says that leaders who stress the importance of luck are just revealing how deeply humble they are. But this isn't humility. It's realism. Those of us who've been blessed to have certain things in our lives play out the way we wanted them to know, on some deep level, that luck was on our side, and that, if things had slipped sideways even just a little, the outcomes could have been very different. There but for the grace of God go I. Or, to quote the poem "If—" by Rudyard Kipling, "If you can meet with Triumph and Disaster and treat those two imposters just the same . . . yours is the Earth and everything that's in it."

Having said this, there are indeed insights and practices that can be gleaned from a study of successful careers. Here are some of the most powerful. Despite the well-intended advice, and pressure from those around you, think about how some of these might apply to you as you craft your own career.

Just Start

How do you know if you've started out right?

You don't. Just start. A career is not a ladder, nor a lattice, nor a jungle gym. A career is a scavenger hunt for love.

Imagine yourself graduating from college and standing at the edge of a forest. There are many openings into the forest. Which one should you take? The "stay in school until you get a master's degree" opening? The "break through the under-brush for a few years and see what you see" opening? The "go to medical school/law school/design school" opening?

Frankly, there's no right answer to this question. So try not to worry about it too much. Just start. Walk into the forest. Any opening will do. And once you're in the forest, keep your mind and heart open to the sight of a red thread—something you love, some activity, or person, or situation where you feel a pull.

After I graduated from college why did I up and leave the UK for Nebraska? Heck, I don't know. All I knew at twenty-one was that there was something about that job and place that intrigued me more than any other job offers I was getting in the center of London.

"What about getting experience elsewhere?" I asked my dad. "Shouldn't I go to some of the biggest companies in Europe and ply my trade there for a while?"

"It's not about experience," Dad said. "It's about the *quality* of the experience. Do you think you'll get something unique and distinct from heading over to Nebraska?"

"Yes," I said.

So I went. Was it the right decision? Could I have experienced greater success and satisfaction by staying closer to home? Maybe. But I'll never know, will I. All I'll know is what occurred on the journey that began with me climbing on a bus to Lincoln.

The same will be true for you. Try not to put too much pressure on yourself to "start out right." Because there is no right start. Or rather, there are a multitude of right starts.

Be generous with yourself. Don't look for a sign to the perfect opening. Don't wait until all the paths have been cut and freed from thick undergrowth and fallen trees. Just start moving. Listen to your instincts, try to find a role in which you might catch a glimpse of a red thread or two, then, as you move down the path, keep your eyes peeled for more red threads.

When you find one, grab hold and follow where it leads.

The "What" Always Trumps the "Who" and the "Why"

In all of my research, it has been crashingly obvious that the most successful people found roles that a) fulfilled their sense of purpose—they believed in the "why" of the role, b) allied them with colleagues they trusted and admired—they connected to the "who" of the role, and c) contained activities they loved—they enjoyed the role's "what."

Happy indeed is the person who finds the beautiful intersection of all three.

But be mindful that of the three, the "what" is the most significant. In study after study, those people who reported that they had a chance to do something they loved each and every day were far more likely to be high performers and to stay in the role than those who reported that they believed in the mission of the company or liked their teammates. It's not that those other two things are unimportant;

it's just that what you are actually being paid to do is more important.

If you believe in the product you're selling, but hate selling, you won't succeed. Likewise, if you greatly admire the members of your team, but find yourself in the wrong role on the team, you will struggle.

So, before you take any job, discipline yourself to investigate exactly what sort of activities will be filling your working week. Find someone who's actually in the role and ask them questions—not whether they love it, since their loves won't necessarily jive with yours. But instead, ask about what specific activities they are doing at 10 a.m. on a regular day at work, or which activities take up the most time on the job. It is these activities that are emotionally charged—either positively or negatively—and if you land in a role where your hours and minutes are filled with activities that drain you, no amount of camaraderie or commitment to mission will compensate. Down this path lies burnout.

And, as the Red Thread Questionnaire will reveal for you, when it comes to the "what," the details matter. When I first started at Gallup, I was delivering results to each person who took one of our strengths assessments, and writing up a report on how this person could grow by leveraging their strengths.

I was pretty good at it. The report writing, I mean. But the activity itself left me cold. I remember calling up the COO of the company, Connie Rath, and saying rather desperately, "I just don't seem to care enough about this particular person. What's wrong with me?"

And she replied, "Nothing's wrong with you. Have you tried presenting? Maybe you're more cut out for communicating in larger groups."

I tried it, and I was.

One-on-one coaching was something I thought I would love. Until I realized I didn't. And so the scavenger hunt continued. A huge thank you to Connie for allowing me to keep scavenging.

You Can Find Red Threads Every Day

As I mentioned in chapter 1, of all the questions the ADP Research Institute has asked during its global studies, the two most powerful in predicting all positive outcomes, whether performance, first-year retention, engagement, or resilience, were these:

Do you have a chance to use your strengths every day?

In the last week, have you felt excited to work every day?

Those who answered "strongly agree" were far more likely to have a boss who reports that "I always turn to this person for outstanding results," far more likely to stick around for more than a year, and far more likely to answer the engagement and resilience items positively.

Notice the words "every day" in each question? These words matter. If you remove them, then these two questions lose *all* their predictive power—meaning the way someone answers them doesn't show any link to all those positive outcomes. The questions don't ask about "all day every day," but they do ask the respondent to own and claim "every day."

What does this mean for you? It means that in terms of your productivity and your psychological well-being, frequency matters. Any day that goes by without you finding something to love, something to get excited about, raises the chance that you will, over time, become less engaged and less productive. No, you won't ever find the perfect job, a job you love 100 percent of the time. You won't ever "do only what you love." But you can—every single day—find some activity or situation or moment or event that you love. It might be the thinnest of red threads, but you can find it.

At least, you can find it if you are deliberate in looking for it. So, begin each morning by spending a few minutes anticipating what the red threads of the day might be. Which instances or activities you think will lift you today. They don't have to be giant lifts—my institute's data has no patterns showing that the people who are supremely excited by work once a quarter are more productive and engaged. When it comes to love, extreme frequency trumps extreme intensity. So discipline yourself to devote a little attention at the beginning of each day to pick out your loves for the day.

In this sense, your enemy here isn't necessarily that you don't have any red threads in your work. Your enemy is distraction. You've stopped paying attention to which moments you love, and so, like all ignored things, those moments have withered and lost their potency.

The antidote here is your attention. Be intentional. Pay attention to the red threads you're going to find at work today, and you'll get from them what you need. Every day.

You Always Have More Power Than You Think

Back in 2008 a very dear friend of mine, B, started to feel numbness in her legs. After suffering through a blitzkrieg of tests, she got a heart-rending diagnosis: ALS. Lou Gehrig's disease. It's a breakdown in the motor neurons that slowly causes the patient to lose control of her muscles. As her husband said at the time, "It's like she's been sentenced to death by slow-motion car crash. Me and the kids have to watch her die, and there's nothing any of us can do about it."

Today, twelve years into a disease that typically kills in three, she is still very much alive. Yes, she can no longer move, or eat, or speak, or even breathe by herself, but she's still in there. And thanks to a fancy machine that can sense where her eyes are focusing, she can communicate to you and me as vividly as she ever could. Each letter has to be selected individually, so for someone as smart and verbal as her, the speed of communication, or lack thereof, must be incredibly frustrating. But at least she can still connect with the rest of us.

In reference to the Covid-19 pandemic, I asked her the other day how she had retained her resilience and spirit. For the last decade she's been doing an extreme version—sheltering in place and social distancing—of what we've been suffering through for over a year and a half. I thought she might be able to teach us something.

> *Marcus, all I can tell you is that I choose to focus on those things I can control. There's so much of my life now that I can't control that if I focused on all I've lost, I would be suicidal by dinnertime. Instead, I focus on what is still within my control. I can still be a good mother to my kids. I can still be a spouse to my husband. I can still be there as a friend.*

As I'm writing this, at this very moment, she's just texted me. I had to put my dog to sleep this week—sweet Marshy, my golden, got pneumonia and I had to make a really tough decision. B's text reads: *T told me you had no option but to put Marshy down. That is such a hard day for you and I am sorry you had to go through that. I remember how he was always a part of your life and how much you loved him. I know you must be devastated, but he adored you, so please hold on to that thought. Sending love as always.*
Imagine how long this one text must have taken for her to construct. While she's lying in her bed, sores on her body, frozen in place, she's not railing against her plight. She's thinking of how I must be feeling this week, and is reaching out to

show her love. She is still right there, and can still be exactly the kind of friend that she ever was.

I bring up B because of course she can teach us something. Your sense of purpose and resiliency stem from your sense of agency. Yes, there's a great deal that you can't control at work. You can't control how your company performs with all its customers, you can't dictate who your boss is, you can't change that daft performance appraisal form, or that certification you're required to take. Start to make a list of all the things at work you can't control, and you'd never stop writing.

Do as my dear friend does, and ignore the list. Instead, focus on what at work you can control. Seventy-three percent of workers say they have the chance to modify their role to fit their strengths better. So start here. Once you've identified one or two red threads, figure out how you can use them to get your work done.

For inspiration, think about the most successful person you know. Not just financially. Someone who appears to have most, if not all, aspects of their work figured out. Someone who, when you look at them, makes you think, *Lucky them. How did they get such a job? It seems to fit them so perfectly. How did they find such a great match?*

The reality, of course, is that they didn't find it. They *made* it. They took a generic job description—as all job descriptions are—and they deliberately and gradually fashioned the job so that it focused more and more on the activities they loved to do. Almost all of us have this room to maneuver. The most successful of us use this room to weave new red threads week by week so that, eventually, the actual work itself is dense with things they love.

No one will ever do this for you, since no one will ever know your red threads as intimately as you do. So it's up to you—no matter what role you find yourself in—to take responsibility for weaving what you love into what you're being paid to do. You, like 73 percent of the workforce, have the power to create the job in your image.

You might start by just focusing on which red threads you know you're going to be able to draw on today.

Then, one week, maybe you figure out how to devote an entire day to one of your reddest threads.

Perhaps, as those Disney housekeepers did by making a little stuffed animal scene for their guests, you can get creative in how a red thread can be woven into a new way of getting your job done.

Perhaps you can sign up for a class that'll help you practice and fine-tune one of your loves.

And then, over time, you might refine your loves into something so distinctive and so powerful that your team is prepared to design a role specifically around you.

As you do this, you may well find that your team and team leader, who were previously neutral to or even obstacles to your success at work, start aligning themselves around you. Others sense something different about you when you are in love with what you're doing—just as the research tells us that people in love are more attractive to others. It's almost as if people can pick up on your elevated levels of oxytocin or norepinephrine.

In your career—as in society at large—change follows the focus of your attention, particularly when you're attentive to what you love.

Never Brag

Whether in interviews, performance reviews, or just regular conversation, you don't need to claim how amazing you are, or how much better than everyone else you are. Most of us find it quite difficult to highlight our qualities while not coming off as a braggart, and so contort ourselves into knots trying to appear humble, while nonetheless trying to leave the other person in no doubt as to our superpowers.

You don't need to contort yourself. Claim specificity rather than superiority. Don't say "I am the best at . . . " Or even the humble-pie version of that.

Use the phrase "I am *at* my best *when* . . . " And then describe in detail the sorts of activities, situations, contexts, and moments that bring out your very best.

"I am at my best when . . . " works really well in job interviews. A version you might want to try when joining a brand-new team is this: "You can always rely on me for . . . " Here again, you aren't claiming superstar performance, you are merely detailing for them the sort of contribution you hope to bring to the team. Not only will you come across as analytical rather than arrogant, but you'll also reveal a capacity for self-mastery. And that's always a gift to any team.

Here are a few more ways you can describe the detail of your Wyrd without bragging:

Over the years, I've found that I . . .

Other people tell me that I . . .

I get a thrill from . . .

I find I learn best when . . .

Some of my best times are when I . . .

Strive to Be Different, Not Complete

One of the strongest forces preventing you from finding what you love is the widely held belief that any job done well requires you to possess a predefined list of attributes and skills. You'll see this in lengthy job descriptions, career paths laid out according to which skills you need for each role, and performance appraisal forms that aim to measure and rate you against the predefined list. The message you're sent is that excelling at a job requires you to be complete, to display all the predefined attributes or skills. If you are seen to be lacking certain ones, then you're encouraged to go acquire the ones you're missing. Then you'll be complete. Then you'll excel.

All of this comes about because someone is trying to bring structure to what's called "workforce planning" or "talent planning." Their efforts are well intended, but are based on the completely false belief that if they can just define all the jobs specifically enough, then they'll be able to select, assess, and train people for these jobs in a predictable and organized way.

The reason this belief is false is that excellence is idiosyncratic—namely, no two people who excel at the same job achieve excellence in the same way. There is no research published in any refereed journal proving that people who excel in the same role—whether they be Navy SEALs, teachers, emergency room nurses, or financial advisers—all possess the same list of skills and attributes. They may well share similar certifications or have passed the same tests, but that's the extent of their sameness. Why they work, how they work, how they build relationships, how they take in information, how they learn, when and why and how they innovate—all of these are unique to each individual.

Unless you happen to be high up in human resources, however, you won't be able to change all the processes that flow from the belief that those who excel in the same job excel in the same way. So, what can you do?

Well, on the surface, you can play the game. Getting rid of job descriptions and job leveling and job competencies is not a hill you need to die on. So, if you want a particular job, it might be sensible to try to show that you match the predefined skill set closely. And if you are preparing for a performance review that includes being rated on competencies, it might be worth thinking about examples that prove you possess all that's supposedly required of you. Luckily, these sorts of things come around only once a year.

But in terms of your real-world success and fulfillment, you'll need to ditch the fakery of appearing complete and instead learn to differentiate.

First, this means learning how to make best use of your red threads. You are a unique individual who finds love in very precise activities, outcomes, and instances. In chapter 8 I shared the Red Thread Questionnaire, which can help you pinpoint the detail of your red threads and differentiate them from all the other threads in the fabric of your life. These red threads are the source of your energy, your learning, and your comparative advantage. You will never be complete. Instead, you will always and forever be weaving these threads into some sort of differentiated contribution.

Second, to differentiate means to become comfortable with describing those threads which are not red. As you've just learned, when you join a new team, you should feel comfortable describing your red threads by saying, "You can always rely on me for . . . " or "I am at my best when . . . "

But you should also learn a technique for describing your threads that aren't red. Here, these sorts of phrases can be helpful:

I'm not at my best when . . .

I find I procrastinate when . . .

I seem to struggle with . . .

I'm drained when . . .

These are simple phrases, but I imagine you haven't used them much at work. Work—because it's built around the myth of completeness—is not a place that encourages you to describe what you don't love. Even though, deep down, you know that you love some activities and loathe others, even though you know that some drain you while others uplift you, and that the difference between these is quite specific, still you will find few venues in which you're encouraged to share this super-important information about you.

What you'll find yourself doing instead is twisting your language around so that you make your weakest threads appear strong. Hence, in job interviews, in response to the inevitable "What are your weaknesses?" question, you'll hear yourself striving to make a gray thread sound red, as in "My weakness is that I care too much" or "My weakness is that my standards are too high."

Try to break yourself of this habit. You won't be able to see and weave your red threads if you spend your life pretending that all your threads are red. Of course, your confessing that some activities drain you or bore you doesn't absolve you of doing them—as the Mayo Clinic research from chapter 6 shows, you don't need an entirely red quilt to excel at what you do. You're not going to love all activities at work, and you're going to have to knuckle down and do them nonetheless. But by clearly differentiating your reds from the rest, you will, over time, become a more trusted teammate. No one trusts a person who loves all they do—just as you don't trust the waiter who, in answer to a question about what's good on the menu, answers "Everything!"

Learn to differentiate, honestly and vividly, between your reds and all the other shades.

You're going to want to apply this to your teammates. Their red threads are as specific and as distinct as your own. To remove frustration from your work life, stop expecting from people what they cannot give. If you've asked a teammate for something more than a couple of times, and they've misunderstood it or haven't delivered it by the deadline or just plain forgot it, then take a hint: this isn't a red thread of theirs. To collaborate well, you need to have some understanding of their threads, and they of yours. The more comfortable you are with sharing your reds and the rest, the more comfortable they'll be in sharing theirs.

This even applies to your team leader. I once worked for a person I was trying to impress by showing her just how many options I'd thought of in terms of next actions. I stayed up all night concocting an uber-detailed PowerPoint of a multiforked flow diagram of if/then possibilities. By morning I'd created something that made NASA's moon landing plans look rather slapdash.

She wasn't impressed at all. Instead, as I began laying out option one of fifteen, she started to shift in her seat, and cut me off with curt questions. Since I'd never seen this from her before, I carried on with my analysis, until she finally erupted with, "Marcus, which one do you think we should do? We need to move on this. By tomorrow."

Her red thread wasn't seeing the multitude of connections and possibilities. It was trusting in her people's opinions, and therefore expecting them to have landed on those opinions before the meeting. Not all leaders share her red thread—and it's not as though this is a leadership thread. In fact, some leaders love detailed contingency planning and possibility thinking. But she didn't. She loved facts, conclusions, and actions.

It took me a while to figure this out—initially, I thought I was constantly letting her down. Boy, that's hard, isn't it. To turn one of your red threads into an actual piece of beautiful work and then have your team leader look at it as barely black and white. Our solution proved to be the same as yours will be should you ever find yourself in a similar situation: share what you love, and ask the other person to do the same. You might not use the "love" word. You might instead use the "I'm at my best when ... " phrase, or, in this case, something like "I can take in information fastest when ... " The goal is to come out of the conversation having described a red thread of yours and having learned a detail or two about theirs.

You're not bragging, nor are you making excuses. You're just trying to see and to be seen so that you can both collaborate better—and that, in the end, is what love at work is all about.

Shape Your Career Like an Hourglass

To begin with, you'll take a job—perhaps any job you can get—and then you'll keep moving, always looking for those activities that seem to be positively charged. You'll spot one red thread, weave it into your current role, then find another, and weave that in as well. Then perhaps a left turn onto a new path, connected to the original one but angling away toward a different part of the forest. Then another turn, another fork, another path.

The early part of your career will probably feel a lot like this. Lots of weaving to and fro, and weaving new threads into the fabric of your understanding of who you are and what you love to do. This is the wide base of the hourglass.

Try not to be too harsh on yourself if you find that, during these first few years of your career, you're searching and searching. If a career is a scavenger hunt for love, then keeping your eyes open for all kinds of possible loves is an intelligent way to begin your hunt.

The Middle of the Hourglass

But after a few years, the research shows, most successful people choose a path and stay on it for a decade or more. They may switch teams or companies or leave the big corporate world entirely during this time, but they stay focused on the same area of expertise.

The most influential research on deep mastery was done by professor K. Anders Ericsson and his team at Florida State University. His data was popularized by the concept of "ten thousand hours"—that if you spend ten thousand hours, roughly ten years, applying yourself to the same thing, you can come to excel at it.

In fact, Ericsson's research didn't lead to this conclusion. He found not that after ten years of focus anyone can excel at anything, but that anyone who ended up getting really good at something had devoted a significant amount of time to their craft. Which is quite different. Your loves, as specific and unique as they are, take time to be channeled into meaningful contribution.

Yes, you may experience rapid learning in some activities— this is one of the signs of love, after all—and yet true expertise in anything, whether selling, housekeeping, engineering, nursing, teaching, marketing, takes years of work. Years in which you try something, experiment with a new approach, and wait for the results—they could come tomorrow, they could come in a year's time, they could drip, drip, drip, one small insight building on the one before, or they could come in one giant burst of insight. But they come over time, and so you learn and build your mastery over time.

This was where Ericsson's work pointed. And if you read the actual research papers, you'll find them thoughtful and methodologically sound. Hippocrates, though, the grandfather of medicine, said pretty much the same thing more than two thousand years ago: "Life is short, the craft is long." We live a good deal longer these days, but his insight is still wise: any craft worth doing is bigger and deeper and richer than one person's lifetime.

So, at some point in your career, you are going to want to honor the path you have chosen—the craft you have chosen—by giving it your extended, undivided attention. Distraction is the enemy of excellence.

And as you do this, you'll gain not only mastery but also credibility. These days everyone seems to be some sort of "thought leader." And the barrier to making content and putting it up on social media platforms has fallen so low that anyone with a phone can opine on anything they like, and we seem to listen—so long as they have thousands of followers, that is.

This kind of follower-driven opining may have value in the world of social media, but it's far less likely to serve you in the world of work. Here you will build the greatest value if you can show yourself to be someone who has stayed focused enough in their field to know all the details, and which details truly matter. Regardless of your field, this sort of expertise is *always* valued on a team. It has heft. It is rare. It is recognized even if other folks on the team don't understand the details themselves. It is intimidating, which is no bad thing. And it leads to you being deeply trusted.

Contrary to what you may have heard or read, being focused in this way doesn't make you narrow, or less open to novelty and innovation. The opposite is true. It is only when you know so well the existing ways of doing things—which ones work, which don't, and when and why—that you are able to imagine what a more effective way might look like. Focus such as this not only helps you anticipate the future—

you are deeper into the forest, further ahead than anyone else, and so can see round more corners—but also helps you create the future. This focus prepares your mind with actions, experiences, and results played out over many years, and as all innovators know, creativity comes *only* to the prepared mind.

Louis Pasteur's exact remark was "In the fields of observation"—which is really all of our fields—"chance favors only the prepared mind." In other words, you've got to know your field in detail before you can notice that the behavior of one particular detail is a sign of something cool and new. In Pasteur's case, it was injecting chickens with an accidentally spoiled batch of chicken cholera and discovering that these particular chickens were then immune to the disease forever. A frustration became an insight about the germ theory of disease, which in turn led to the discovery of vaccination to prevent disease.

In your case, it might be an insight into a more effective way to reduce post-op pain in your patients. Or a slightly better way to explain calculus to a student with specific learning differences. Or a breakthrough in how a certain sports fabric can be constructed to transmit moisture away from the skin. Or how to word a marketing email so that the open rate doubles. But whatever your craft, once you've scavenged around for a few years, and tied a few red threads together, hold on, keep weaving them into an ever-thickening rope, and you'll see your mastery, your creativity, and your value grow exponentially over time.

The Top of the Hourglass

And then perhaps—and it is "perhaps" because many people choose to stay on the mastery path their entire career—you can branch out and become responsible for many other people, on many other paths. This is the widening at the top of the hourglass.

Here your own mastery serves as the foundation for your ability to lead others.

This is because people follow a leader only when they see something that will turn anxiety about the future into confidence. Your mastery is, to other people, confidence-inducing. It shows them something specific and tangible about you, something vivid, not vague. It shows them that you are both an expert in who you are—and therefore who you will be no matter what situations you all encounter—and an expert in your chosen craft—and therefore are more likely to see around corners and be ready for whatever the future might hold for them. Both of these inspire confidence.

In our book *Nine Lies About Work*, Ashley Goodall and I referred to this leader quality as a "spike," as in "the best leaders are spiky"—meaning they have devoted themselves to getting really good at something that matters to their followers. And this mastery, this focused combination of love and work, is the source of their ability to lead others. You know this intuitively—think of any leader, any person you would follow willingly, and they are vivid in your mind. Their characteristics, their deep expertise, their way of decision making, all of these are super-defined. This leader may not be perfect, and you neither want nor expect them to be. But they are precise—and this is why people follow them. Warren Buffett is not Richard Branson is not Margaret Thatcher is not Martin Luther King Jr. is not Desmond Tutu is not Jacinda Ardern is not Vladimir Putin—they're imperfect, they're different, and they're all super-spiky.

If you don't trust your intuition on this, there's some research coming out of Cisco that'll confirm it for you. In a very cleverly designed experiment, Cisco researchers surveyed thousands of employees about their views on their work and the company, and then, at a separate time, they asked these employees to come up with words or phrases to describe their team leader. Some leaders had a wide variety of descriptors, almost as if the team members were unsure about who the leader really was. Whereas other leaders generated descriptors that all zeroed in on the same few attributes. These leaders were more defined in the eyes of their team. They were spiky.

Then, using some very fancy math and natural language processing algorithms, the researchers discovered that of all the survey questions they asked team members, the one that led to the highest ratings on the spiky leaders' teams was this one: "I have great confidence in the company's future."

The takeaway for you is that all the time you spend in the middle of the hourglass is vital if you ever want to thrive as a leader at the top of the hourglass. Honor your craft with years of attention, and you will not only become better at your craft, but you will become more defined and thus more confidence-inducing in the minds of your followers.

Of course, by giving your craft years of focus, you'll also be modeling for them that you have empathy for their own search for mastery. That you deeply value mastery. That you will be patient. That you will give them the time they need to take their loves seriously, just as you did. That you are dismissive of dilettantes, not fooled by follower-fame, and appreciate, above all, that the craft is long.

This is what we all want from our leaders.

Love @ Work

How to Become a Love + Work Leader

L
ate in the fall of 2017, on the Indonesian island of
Sulawesi, Pak Hamrullah, a local anthropologist,
discovered what scientists now believe is the earliest
human art. Conservatively, it could date back forty-four thousand years, though more than likely it's much older. Walking
through a limestone cave, Pak caught sight of a small opening
above him. He clambered up a fig tree and crawled inside it.
There on the wall, illuminated by the light of his cell phone,
he saw a painting. Five meters in length and drawn in red pig-
ment, the painting depicted a small group of humans holding either spears or ropes and, close by, a number of animals
indigenous to the region—a deer, an anoa, a wild pig. It's a
hunting scene. The small band of humans is trying to capture
or kill the animals.

That Pak had found such an ancient depiction of a hunt
was extraordinary enough, but even more intriguing was

how the human figures were drawn. Though clearly meant to be people, each had been given an animal head, or a tail, or both. Anthropologists call these half-human, half-animal figures *therianthropes* and took their presence in the hunting scene to be proof that forty-four thousand years ago we humans were already creating mythological figures. Perhaps this scene revealed the dawning of religious belief.

And perhaps it does. But in reading about the Sulawesi cave paintings, I was struck by a different interpretation. Each of these human-like figures must have been given different animal characteristics for a reason. Possibly each figure wasn't mythological at all, but was instead a real person, someone the painter actually knew, and she (anthropologists believe most prehistoric cave art was made by women) had given each one the distinct animal features that best described their distinctive human traits. The tail of a crocodile to denote intelligence. The wings and beak of a bird to celebrate speed. A lion's head for courage.

The earliest human painting we've yet found is a painting of a team. A team in which each member shares the same goal, but also brings their unique qualities to support the rest of the team.

I don't know about you, but I find this interpretation of the painting greatly comforting. From the earliest prehistoric times we have realized how different we are from one another, how much we rely on one another, and how we can achieve so much more together than we ever can alone. We humans are, and have always been, team creatures. Work is teamwork.

Back in 2019, as I and my ADP Research Institute team were analyzing the data from our global study of the world's workers, we discovered just how pervasive and powerful "work is teamwork" remains today. Workers who reported that they felt part of a team were not only 2.7 times more likely to be fully engaged, they were three times more likely to be highly resilient and two times more likely to report a strong sense of belonging to their organization.

It sounds obvious to stress how vital teams are to all human endeavor, and yet look closer and you'll see that when you are taught about teams, the point is that you, the individual, are not as important as the team: "There is no I in team." Teamwork is introduced as an aspiration to remind you that you yourself are less than the whole.

As Pak's painting reveals, this is a complete misunderstanding of the point of a team. We did not invent teams to remind individuals that they are not as important as the group. We created teams precisely because it was the best mechanism for maximizing the unique qualities of each individual. We sat around the fire, pondering how the heck we were going to solve our problems—building shelter, finding our way, taking down animals far bigger than each of us—and we peered through the smoke at our uniquely gifted brothers and our sisters. In one we saw the talent for organization, in another the instinctive connection to animals, in another brute strength, in another cunning, and we thought to ourselves, *What if we combined these different people into a unit, these four fingers into a fist.*

And so we spoke to our brothers and sister around the fire, we told them of the hill that we needed to take, and then described how each one could play their part, together.

"There is no I in team" misses the mark. The entire point of a team is to capitalize on each "I." I's, coordinated, are what a team is. Teams are the perfect place for you to both celebrate and contribute your unique loves.

Organizations have created such disengaging places to work precisely because they haven't understood the power of teams. If you are not part of a team, our data shows, less than 10 percent of you feel engaged, resilient, and connected. This goes some way to explaining why we learned that health care workers and educators are the two least engaged and least resilient professions: neither hospitals nor schools have been organized around teams.

To contribute your best at work, you'll have to buck this teamless working world. How can you do this? How can you seek out a team where your colleagues and your leader are deeply interested in who you are and what you bring to the team?

As I described at the beginning of the book, many organizations impose on you processes and tools that appear to have been designed to deliberately distance you from who you really are. Your unique loves, your uniqueness in general, runs counter to the organization's need for uniformity—of products, services, even values—and so the goal of work is experienced by you as an ongoing effort to make you as much as possible like every other salesperson, housekeeper, teacher, manager, nurse, machinist, or whatever your role might be.

Wrongheaded though this is, you're not going to be able to recreate your organization's talent management practices all by yourself. Yes, folks like me and others are trying to influence your leaders to throw out these uniformity-focused talent practices in favor of more individualized ones, but this will take a few years. What can you do in the meanwhile? You want to find love in your work, you want to be seen for your whole, authentic self at work, and for the very best of you. How can you pull this off, when so many of the tools and technologies and processes at work are trying—well intendedly—to smother you?

And indeed, some of your fellow humans at work might be trying to do the same. Work is an ecosystem that, yes, includes you—but it also includes your teammates, your team leader, your senior leaders, and your HR department. Where does love fit into this ecosystem? How can you lead a super-productive, high-performing team with love?

First, try to get your thinking right, and then, whether you are a team member, team leader, or senior leader, you can follow the actions that flow from the thinking. To help you, here are five myths and truths to guide you in becoming a Love + Work leader.

MYTH: The team leader should set goals at the beginning of the year.

TRUTH: The team leader should check in with each team member for fifteen minutes every week.

Goals are tricky. They are one of the most common characteristics of your working world, and yet they're also one of the
least loving. They don't have to be loveless. In your nonwork
world, goals serve as a way to make real the loves you feel
inside you. When I set myself a goal of getting into that room
with Don Clifton, it was because I felt I loved what he was
doing in that room. The goal started inside me as a love, and
then I externalized it as a goal. This is the way goals will work
in your life as well. Goals don't have to be measurable, or specific, or time-bound, they just have to come from within you.
Any goal springing from your loves is a good and useful thing.

Unfortunately, this is not how we see them used in the world
of work. Instead, they are usually deployed from on high, with
your senior leaders defining goals for the entire organization,
and then cascading these down through every level until you
get yours. For the organization itself, goal-setting at this high
level is no bad thing—each department head needs to budget for the coming year, and revenue and profitability targets
serve as a good way to project into the future so that sensible
investment decisions can be made for each department.

The problem with goals comes when they land upon your
head. These goals were not set by you. They did not spring
from what you love. In fact, they are ignorant of and irrelevant to what you love. They are, as we described in *Nine Lies
About Work*, un-goals.

You don't necessarily need to pick a public fight with them,
though. Despite how blind they are to your loves, these corporate goals are most likely going to be around for a while,

at least until we all get a little more data-fluent and discover that using goals to rate someone's performance or determine someone's pay is a gross misuse of data. The difficulty of my goals doesn't match yours, and besides, even if they did, your team leader and mine differ in how they assess our progress toward these goals. Basically, all goal-attainment data is systematically invalid and shouldn't be used to evaluate anybody.

But, as I said, getting this realization widespread enough to spare you the yearly bump of goals dropping from the ceiling is going to take a few more years. While you're waiting, here's a new ritual you can do with your team leader, or as a team leader if you are one already. It's called a check-in, and happily it can coexist with cascaded corporate goals. And it's free.

A check-in is a fifteen-minute conversation that you have with your team leader each week about your upcoming week. This conversation is built on your answers to four short questions, two about last week, two about this week:

What activities did I love last week?

What activities did I loathe last week?

What are my priorities this week?

What help do I need from you, my team leader?

This check-in seems so simple but it contains within it all the nuances of how you want to turn your loves into contribution at work. Each week, while your memory is still fresh, you get to think about and share a couple of red threads, and maybe a few of other shades. You don't have to talk in vague theoretical terms, such as "I loved helping people." Instead, you can get right to the detail of "I loved working through that accounting error with Malcolm in prep for that budget meeting."

A check-in is akin to doing a short-form Red Thread Questionnaire each week, and then sharing it immediately with your team leader.

And then, of course, this sharing is not put on a shelf or stuffed into a report somewhere. It's immediately applied to what you're working on in the coming week, and what help you might need from your boss. On one level, what's useful about this is that you and your boss will stay connected and aligned as all the inevitable changes in the real world tumble down upon you both. The rigid goals that you entered into your performance management software at the beginning of the year, and that were irrelevant by the third week of the year, are replaced by a regular, weekly check-in to ensure that you and your work are lined up right.

On another level, though, what's great about a check-in is that it keeps you paying attention to your loves and how you're applying them week by week. Burnout, like bankruptcy or falling asleep, happens gradually and then suddenly. A check-in serves as a pressure-release valve. Yes, you may well have some weeks where you find precious few red threads. And yes, during those loveless weeks you and your team leader may just have to agree that you need to push through. But at least you now know that you're going to be able to start feeling the pull of some red threads soon, maybe not next week, but the week after. And most importantly, you know that your team leader knows where you're at. There's something very comforting and therefore powerful in knowing that *they* know what *you* know about yourself, your loves, and your work.

In trying to persuade your team leader to establish a check-in routine with you, here's some data that'll help:

- Those team leaders who check in every week drive their team members' engagement scores up 77 percent, and their team members' voluntary turnover in the next six months down 67 percent.

- It doesn't matter whether the check-in happens in person, by phone, by email, or in an app. What matters is simply that it happens.

- Leaders who wind up actually having this interaction with the team member about the four questions/answers drive statistically higher levels of performance and engagement in their team members. Here, too, it doesn't matter if the interaction is voice to voice or text to text.

- Ratings of quality don't seem to matter: even if you and your team leader don't have a genius coaching moment during one check-in, don't worry about it. You're going to check in again next week, and maybe something will strike both of you then. What matters with a check-in is that it happens frequently, not necessarily that it happens brilliantly. When it comes to leading, frequency trumps quality.

If you are yourself a team leader, it will serve you well to establish the check-in as one of your core rituals, what General Electric calls your standard leader behaviors. Think about it not as something you do *in addition* to leading. The check-in *is* leading. It is linking the person's loves to the work they are being tasked to do, every week, for the entire year.[1] This is what leaders do. If the thought of checking in with each person bores you—if it's a gray thread of yours—then you should definitely think twice about becoming a leader. For a leader, checking in is akin to brushing teeth. It's just what you do, all the time, a nonnegotiable.

To be clear, this doesn't mean that you are checking *up* on your people—there's no love in that. Instead, you are doing the most loving thing possible—you are seeing the person, right now, for who they are and what they are doing. You are paying them attention. And the more you check in with your people, the more love-filled your team will be, and so the more productivity, creativity, resilience, and collaboration you will get.

If you think that you'd love to check in with each of your team members, but you can't because you've got too many people, well, then you've got too many people. The perfect span of control for you, the team leader, isn't actually a function of control. It's a function of how many people you can pay attention to each week. *Span of control* should be renamed *span of attention*.

If you can't give each person weekly attention in some disciplined way, some way that starts with them and their answers, then you will be driving love out of your workplace, with all of the negative repercussions that come with it. If you build a hospital where the nurse-supervisor-to-nurse ratio is one to forty, then the poor supervisors will be unable to check in with each nurse, the nurses will feel unseen and unheard, and will then, as we've seen, burn out. The same applies to schools, or distribution centers, or call centers, or manufacturing plants. Anywhere we've built reporting structures that prevent weekly check-ins, we should expect to see far higher levels of accidents on the job, workers comp claims, lost workdays, and ninety-day turnover, and lower levels of quality and customer satisfaction. And we do.

On a brighter note, if we want to reduce all those negative employee outcomes and increase the positive ones, then the check-in is the simplest and most powerful prescription. Make it your standard leader behavior, and you'll bring love back into the workplace.

MYTH: Growth comes from analyzing and eliminating blind spots.

TRUTH: Growth comes from learning about love.

> If I create from the heart, nearly everything works; if from the head, almost nothing.
>
> —Marc Chagall

Your loves are not something to be proud of. There's nothing inherently good or bad, or noble or ignoble, about your loves. All they are is a power source. What is good, what is noble, is when you take them seriously and use them to create outcomes for the benefit of others. This doesn't just happen though, does it. It usually requires help from someone else, someone who can help you step back from yourself and show you those little sparks of love. You know what they *feel* like, but someone else can show you what they *look* like, and the effect they've had on others.

So, in some of your check-ins, push the conversation toward something you loved this week that felt like it really worked. You're not doing this to get a pat on the head, but rather, as the glorious painter Marc Chagall confessed, you're doing it so that you can make more things, better things. You're doing it so that you can innovate.

If you are a team leader, try to become known for being really curious about what your people love. You might start with recognition by saying, "Hey, well done on that project last week," but you won't stop there. You'll keep asking questions:

Was that fun for you?

What did you love most about it?

Did you learn anything new, any flashes of insight?

We've got another similar project coming up. Anything you want to tweak or change this time around?

You're not trying to answer these questions yourself, of course. Even though you may be more experienced than your team member, you don't share their precise red threads, and so all you're trying to do is nudge them back into the middle of the activity that they loved. This way you aren't the teacher inhibiting your student with your preset answers. You are the curious catalyst, using your attention to allow the person to come up with answers and insights that, frankly, you'd never have come up with yourself.

If I'd been Ashley's team leader in chapter 12, I never would have thought to tell him to imagine that audiobook reading was akin to piano sight-reading. And yet his discovery was absolutely perfect for him and led to outstanding performance. When I tried to data-dump from my brain to his, as Chagall said, nothing worked. When Ashley let his heart flow, everything did.

MYTH: You can love your people too much.

TRUTH: More love is always better.

Is calling for love-filled workplaces too soft? Will it lead to an inability to deal head-on with poor performance? Is it appropriate to speak of love when, on some occasions, it becomes necessary for organizations to lay off those they "love"? After the #MeToo movement opened a window onto exploitation at work and finally let the light shine in, is it inappropriate and even dangerous to speak of love at work?

To love someone is to see them, all of them, the best of them, to accept what you see, and then to do everything in your power to help them be the biggest version of themselves. Your love is expectant, it wants the other person to take seriously the unique loves they feel, and then turn them into contribution. Your love is insightful and kind, intimate and individualized and inspiring. It can lift up the other person to flights of performance and creativity they never dreamed of.

But no, it is not soft. It is the antithesis of soft. Your love for another can't stand the idea that they are not living into all they could be. Your love will challenge them, and cajole them, and never leave them be, and if, at some point, you see them heading in a direction that will hurt them, or shrink them, you will push them out of harm's way, even if they themselves can't yet see the love in what you're doing. If you love someone, you do for them what is right for them, not necessarily what they want. You are demanding, your expectations are the highest of the high.

This is tough love. Sometimes at work you will be called upon to bring it. And when you do, you better bring it from a place of love, from wanting to help people, because tough love without the love is either clinical or brutal. No workplace wants that.

What of romantic love in the workplace? It happens quite a lot, doesn't it. Depending on which research survey you reference, 22 to 27 percent of us met our partner through work and more than half of us would consider dating someone at work. When Michelle Robinson was asked out on a date by her newly hired college intern, she resisted for a few weeks—*How tacky is that!* she thought. Obviously, not so tacky that she didn't relent, and wind up falling in love with him. She and Barack Obama will soon celebrate their thirtieth wedding anniversary. Bill Gates met Melinda French while she was a manager at Microsoft. Sheryl Sandberg met her current fiancé when Facebook hired his firm to do global branding work. UK Prime Minister Boris Johnson met his fiancée through work. Work is where Eva Mendes met her partner, Ryan Reynolds his, Natalie Portman hers. Myshel Romans hers.

Work can be a place where each of you gets to see the other's full fabric, all those beautiful threads. It's not surprising. It is actually a lovely, human thing, which I doubt we could stop no matter how hard we tried.

This doesn't mean that we can't be thoughtful about how we navigate romantic relationships in the workplace. Not having two partners in a reporting relationship seems quite sensible. Some organizations require both parties to sign a "relationship agreement" to reduce liability should the relationship break down. This also has merit, in the same way that a prenup has merit—not quite my cup of tea, but I can see some organizations requiring it to reduce risk. Likewise, I can see why a no-hugging policy might be sensible for some organizations.

No matter your organization's policies, remember that love is about seeing and being seen, and wanting the other person to be bigger. At its core it is, of course, deeply respectful. When Myshel, while working at her previous company, walked into the training room supply closet to get materials for her next class and turned around to find her boss, with whom she had built a two-year professional relationship, exposing himself, this was the opposite of respect. When, upon being rebuffed, her boss cut her out of all subsequent decisions and shunned her at work, this was the opposite of respect. The hundreds of thousands of women and men and trans and gender nonconforming team members who have experienced similar—and far worse—abuse, they too have been disrespected. Exploited. Overpowered. Unseen.

Whatever word you want to use, whatever the specifics of their experience, it was not loving. It was the opposite of love. More love in the workplace means more respect, more team members seeing the whole other person, more elevating of each other no matter what they look like, how they think, or whom they love.

Love is not like oxygen. You can never have too much of it.

MYTH: Your organization's culture comes from the top.

TRUTH: Your organization's culture comes from the teams.

If you want to learn about the love in your workplace, then don't look to what your organization says about itself online. Don't read about its culture. Don't ask about work-life balance in your job interview. Well, you can, but don't expect to learn anything real about whether your organization takes your own personal loves seriously.

This is because, despite what you may hear from your senior executives, your organization's culture doesn't come from the top. What comes from the top is the organization's talent brand. They use the word "culture," but really they are just trying to be as attractive as possible to the best talent out there. This is no bad thing. In a tight labor market, it is smart to make some specific and differentiated—and true—statements about what the organization does to treat its talent well.

However, the reality of what it's like to work in the organization is always and only a function of your fellow team members and your team leader. The data on this is unequivocal. If you try to find any data showing that a particular organization has created an experience for employees that is uniform across the organization and quantitatively different from other organizations', you will struggle to find any at all. Instead, as we described in *Nine Lies About Work*, what the data shows is that measures of what it is like to work in any organization vary the most *inside* the organization, among all the different teams.

So, to know if your organization is indeed deeply interested in the uniqueness of your loves, begin your job interview process by asking to speak to your team leader. Ask them what their span of control is, how frequently they meet with each team member individually, and then, if you can, find the right moment to ask them to describe a couple of individual team members. Ask what motivates each team member, how each learns, what kind of praise or recognition each one prefers.

All you are listening for here is vivid detail. Obviously, you won't know if the team leader is accurate in what they're describing, but assessing accuracy isn't the point. The point is to pin your ears back and see whether your soon-to-be manager is the kind of leader who's interested enough in each person to learn about their different loves.

And then, if you can, try to arrange a brief conversation with other team members. Ask them how frequently they meet one-on-one with the boss, and if the team leader knows them well. Again, whatever they share, believe what you're hearing. And if it sounds like the span of control is too large, or that the leader doesn't check in much, doesn't know them well, then you might still take the job. But if you do, know that you'll have to make your contribution to the team without the benefit of the manager's attention. Which is possible, but only for a brief stint. Your long-term growth always requires the attention of those around you.

MYTH: The organization's most valuable asset is its people.

TRUTH: The organization's most valuable asset is its trust.

Since 2015, I and my research teams have surveyed workers in twenty-five countries. We've analyzed over a million StandOut strengths assessments, and recorded more than four million check-ins. And if you were to ask me, today, what is the single most reliable finding from this research, I would share this:

We asked people if they trusted their teammates, their team leader, and their senior leaders. Those who strongly agreed that they trusted two of these three groups were three times more likely to be fully engaged and highly resilient. Those who strongly agreed that they completely trusted all three groups were *fifteen* times more likely to be fully engaged and *forty-two* times more likely to be highly resilient.

Trust is just everything. Without trust you can't usher love into your organization. So, if you are a team member, *anything* you do to build trust with your colleagues will be a step in the right direction to bringing love—and all the good stuff that comes with it—into your workplace. Keep people's confidences; do what you say you're going to do; risk with others; share your red threads and the other shades, too; be individualized in how you assess others; be generous in your explanation of their actions.

If you are a team leader, you too must be a bringer of trust into your team. Do your check-ins each week; make few and small commitments and keep them all; never talk negatively about one team member to another; always do for people what is right for them even if that is not always what they want; share in detail with each one what you have come to see and learn about them. These are the sorts of actions that, little by little, build trust on your team and bring love in.[2]

And if you are a senior leader, what can you do to establish such a level of trust that a true Love + Work organization emerges? Certainly, all of the actions above apply to you, too—you are a team member and a leader of your team before you are a leader of teams of teams. But what of the broader organization? What can you do to usher love in?

You can start by stopping certain rituals:

- The Love + Work organization doesn't cascade goals down from on high—because goals imposed from above interfere with each person thinking through what they love and how they can contribute it.

- The Love + Work organization doesn't use performance ratings—because no one trusts ratings. They reduce each person to a fabricated number and prevent the organization from seeing the whole person.

- The Love + Work organization doesn't use any performance feedback tools—because these tools diminish trust. Others' feedback reveals them and obscures you. Their feedback is blind to what you love.

- The Love + Work organization doesn't do cascaded talent reviews—because these degrade trust across the entire organization. No one feels comfortable knowing that, three levels up, a group of people who don't know them are talking about them, their level of "completeness," and how this level should affect their future in the organization.

- The Love + Work organization doesn't conduct centralized employee opinion surveys—these remove trust from where it should be located: the team. All employee opinion surveys, if they happen, should be launched by the team leader and the results given back to the team and the team leader first.

What, then, should you do instead?

Below are the characteristics of what Love + Work organizations do. I was wondering how to share them with you since few of us are in the kind of position where we can design our organization from the ground up. I'll present them as though you're asking about them in a job interview. As a person with loads of talent, you are a precious commodity. All kinds of organizations will want you. So, whether or not it is apparent to you, you do have quite a lot of power to change the practices and policies at work. You can start by asking about the characteristics of a Love + Work organization in your job interview, and then, to exercise some measure of your power, you can reject any organization that doesn't have them. I realize that this will require both discipline and courage from you—if the company is offering you a significant salary, or a coveted avenue for growth, then it's going to be hard to take a stand. But think about the next person behind you, and the next; think about your friend you care about, your cousin, your brother or sister. If you vote with your feet and reject any organization that doesn't meet these Love + Work criteria, then you will potentially be one of many. If we get enough talented people like you choosing to join only those organizations which are committed to taking each employee's loves seriously, then together we'll be able to affect great change at work.

The Love + Work Organization Interview

Questions 1–5 are the minimum requirements. Think twice about joining an organization that doesn't meet them.

Questions 6–11 are higher-order characteristics. If you find an organization that embodies these, you're potentially looking at a special sort of workplace, one that has dedicated itself to helping you thrive.

Minimum Love + Work Requirements: 1–5

1. What is the organization's mission?

This is a straightforward one, but it's nonetheless a good place to start since the best leaders don't cascade goals, they cascade meaning. So push for answers that bring this meaning to life. You're listening for vivid examples, stories, recent anecdotes. Keep your ears peeled for vague platitudes—"We care about our people, we strive to be the best, we love our customers." When you hear these, always push for specific examples. A true Love + Work organization would be able to share with you what it is passionate about, and help you link what you love to this broader passion.

2. How many direct reports does the CEO have?

You're looking for a number below ten. Everything good, or bad, starts at the top. The CEO is first and foremost a team leader. If they have more than ten direct reports, then it's a sign that they do not take seriously each team member's need for frequent, future-focused attention. (Don't be fobbed off with: Well, at this level, our ExCom members don't need such frequent attention. This is akin to saying: Well, at this level, our ExCom members have ceased to be human. Which is either wrong or scary.)

3. What kind of formal team-joining program do you offer?

If they have no idea what you are talking about, this is a bad sign. If they say, "We leave this up to each team leader," this is also a bad sign. According to meta-analyses, most new recruits know within the first ninety days whether they have made the right decision about joining a new organization, and by far the strongest real-world predictor of whether they will stay or leave is whether they feel part of a team. A Love + Work organization would know this, and would have developed a formal team-joining program to address it.

4. How frequently will I meet with my team leader to discuss my priorities and performance one-on-one?

You are listening for "every single week." Listen closely. What you hear is what you will actually get. More than likely you'll hear something about "every week as a team" or "as many times as you would like." Ignore these deflection responses, and instead try to zero in on whether the organization makes it a priority for team leaders and team members to talk frequently, one-on-one, about near-term future work.

5. Does the organization support my ongoing education in any way?

Obviously, you are looking for a yes. It almost doesn't matter what the program is. It could be paying for advanced degrees, co-paying for ongoing education, helping with student loans, offering the famed Google "20 percent personal project time"—anything that shows the organization sees you as a work in progress, an entity whose learning and growing is a moral imperative, independent of what the organization might benefit from in the short term.

Higher-Order Love + Work Characteristics: 6–11

6. What does the organization do to build more teams like its best teams?

This is a tough one. What you are listening for is, frankly, anything at all. Even though humans have been working in teams for fifty thousand years, most organizations still don't make it a priority to study which teams work best and why. If leaders have done *anything* deliberate to understand what their best teams do differently, or what the characteristics of their best teams are, take it as a sign that they realize "so goes the team, so goes the organization." Doesn't really matter what they found. What matters is that they were asking the right questions.

7. Do you have career paths defined by required competencies?

In psychometrics this is called a *negatively coded item*, meaning you are listening for: no, we think jobs should be defined by a few simple outcomes, not prescribed competencies. Red flag if they say yes.

8. Do you have any sort of peer-feedback system?

Another negatively coded item. You definitely want to hear: no.

9. Will I have an HR generalist dedicated to me/people in my same role?

Here you are listening for a resounding yes. The most recent research by the ADP Research Institute reveals that employees who have a single HR point of contact are much more likely to recommend the organization to friends and family. Which makes sense when you think about it. Everything that HR deals with—from pay, to vacations, to leaves of absence, to career paths—is fraught with the unique needs and circumstances of each team member. If the organization is taking these unique needs seriously, then it will ensure that you have an HR "quarterback" who will get to know you, your family, your loves, fears, hopes, and dreams. Sadly, most organizations have done away with this. Instead, they've created vertical tracks of expertise—compensation, benefits, vacation, and so on—and call centers to handle all the inbound questions for each, leaving you in the middle to try to navigate it all. As with the patient who feels as though each medical specialist knows a bit of them but no doctor seems to know all of them, this multiple-track HR system is unnerving. A true Love + Work organization would start with you, the whole individual, and then build its system out from there.

10. Does the organization have an alumni program of any kind?

This one will stump most organizations, but it's significant. The point here is that a Love + Work organization would see you through the lens of not just your current employment, but also your lifelong growth and contribution. As in: "You and your contribution to the world are the moral and ethical point of everything, and so we will not see you as having value only while you are employed with us. Instead, we will find ways to stay in touch with you, so that we can see how your work with us helped you find and contribute your loves to the world." Yes, of course, as McKinsey, Accenture, and many others have found, a strong alumni association yields many other shorter-term business benefits in the form of client relationships, industry connections, and marketplace talent brand. But a Love + Work organization isn't doing it for those reasons alone. It's staying close to alumni because they—their loves, their potential, their contribution—are the ultimate morality.

The Love + Work Interview

1. What is the organization's mission?

2. How many direct reports does the CEO have?

3. What kind of formal team-joining program do you offer?

4. How frequently will I meet with my team leader to discuss my priorities and performance one-on-one?

5. Does the organization support my ongoing education in any way?

---

6. What does the organization do to build more teams like its best teams?

7. Do you have career paths defined by required competencies?

8. Do you have any sort of peer-feedback system?

9. Will I have an HR generalist dedicated to me/people in my same role?

10. Does the organization have an alumni program of any kind?

11. How do you offboard team members?

11. *How do you offboard team members?*

This is an odd one to ask in a job interview, but ask it anyway. What you are listening for is any program that reveals how deeply the organization respects the fears, needs, and loves of team members leaving the organization. Their loves do not end just because their employment does. Any true Love + Work organization would recognize this and lead people out with as much love and respect as they bring people in. Listen very carefully. At some point, you and your loves might be walking out that door, and you'll want to know whether the company sees your value as a human continuing when you do.

Love in Learning

Why It Is Missing and How You Can Get It Back

When are we going to change the schools?

For the last thirty years, I've given presentations on how the power of human nature is that each human's nature is unique. How each of us has different loves and loathes and strengths and passions, and the best way for us to grow is to channel our uniqueness into something productive.

And it's a rare day when someone does *not* come up afterward and say some version of, "Why don't we do this with our kids in school?"

Each of us knows we are unique, that there is no one in the world quite like us, and we instinctively feel that school should be a place that talks to us about what makes us unique, that helps us understand it, and honor it, and apply it toward our own learning. We want to let school in, let the lessons get under our skin, and feel ourselves growing into the best versions of ourselves, from the inside out, as it were.

For most of us, though, school does not feel like this—and the impact this has on who we are as adults is profound. School feels like something being done to us. It doesn't get to know us much at all, throws facts and lessons and exams and grades at us, and leaves us to withstand the onslaught. School can soon become something to beat back, something to fight against and win, a strange land of unnatural customs, bizarre rituals, and endless judgment.

We try to learn just enough of this alien world to survive, to climb the rungs put in front of us, always keeping our heads low, our eyes down on our assignments and quizzes, so that we can secure for ourselves the precious passports out of this world: a good GPA, high scores on the ACT and SAT, and the right listing of extracurricular activities.

Sadly for us, our climb out of school just leads to college and a job, both of which turn out to be built around the same bizarre set of rituals: learning as information transfer, someone else judging our performance, someone else identifying our gaps and telling us to plug those gaps in order to improve our performance rating and so get promoted.

This whole procession—from primary school through high school, college, and work—pressures us to separate us from ourselves. Little wonder that students drug themselves up to push their anxiety down; parents go to ridiculous, even illegal lengths to give their kids the right scores and credentials; organizations fail to engage even 20 percent of their workforce. The entire ecosystem appears rigged against each one of us.

In 2019 I got an unwanted front-row seat to what this pressure does to parents, and to their kids. I'm still trying to make sense of what happened, as are my kids, and I imagine we will be doing so for the rest of our lives. I share it with you now not because I have all the answers as to what exactly caused this scandal. Nor to pass judgment on those who were involved.

I share it simply because the intensity of the pain created in me an urgency and a passion to make change. I'm hoping that my and my kids' experiences might create similar feelings in you. Because yes, absolutely, we need to come together—as students, parents, teachers, and administrators—and demand change in our schools.

"What's Going to Happen Now, Dad?"

We love our kids more than life itself, don't we. When they feel pain, we feel it fifty times over. I had pain as a child. I'm sure you did too. Much of my pain I strategically buried or found a good bunker for. I'm sure you did too. We figure it out and keep going. But when we see our children in pain, it's almost unbearable. You're sliced open, raw, and for many of us it is then and only then that we ask for help.

My son is my utter everything. My firstborn. I pulled him up next to my heart to hold him for the first time on a frigid New York morning in March 2001. It was so beautifully disorienting, holding a life we'd created. He was a little ball of magic, grasping on tight to his umbilical cord as he cried and squirmed and wiggled. And I was full like never before. Bursting. A human I had never known instantly became the human I loved most.

What I wanted for him then is what all of us want for our kids: to have a chance to express the very best of himself and to be seen for who he truly is, in all of his quirky magnificence. I wanted the world to know him.

Eighteen years later, again in March, I pulled him up next to my heart to hug him. Now he felt lifeless. His voice monotone and flat. He drew back, looked at me desolately, and walked away. The whites of his eyes were gray. He sat down on the wood floor with his shoulders turned in to his knees. It was as if he had no oxygen flowing through his lungs. Or maybe I had none.

That morning, March 12, 2019, I became the father of a son who had innocently found himself a headline in one of the biggest college cheating scandals of our time.

The call came in at 6:35 a.m. "Dad, are you at your house?" his voice shivered.

"Yes," I replied.

"You need to come here," he said. "Mom's been arrested by the FBI."

I stood there outside my garage about to head to work, trying to make sense of what I'd just heard. The jasmine on the garage walls was blooming, and I will forever associate their sweet smell with panic. My son's words weren't real life. Sure, my ex and I had had a high-conflict divorce, and yes, sadly, we didn't speak to each other, but she was in no way a venal character. She was the opposite, a Captain Marvel type, ready and willing to step in and save the day, the anti-flake, the parent who knew everything. The idea that she would be arrested by the Federal Bureau of Investigation simply didn't compute.

The fifteen-minute drive to their house feels like three hours and no time at all, as my palms slip on the shifter.

I pull up to their house, open my car door, look up, and catch the disapproving eye of the neighbor next door out walking his perfect brown labradoodle. The gate is hanging open and I trip over the front steps in my haste to get to the door. Hunched over, a wave of nausea hits me, and I stop. The labradoodle barks, and I straighten myself up with a big breath of air. I know I have to show strength in the face of whatever I am about to walk into.

My two kids are both sitting on the wooden floors in the hall. Maybe it's because it used to be my home and hasn't been for a while, or maybe it's just that morning, but as I walk in it doesn't feel like a home that people live in. It feels to me as though they are moving house, or as if someone has just died. I stay in the hall talking to them, but my sense is that if I opened any of the doors to the other rooms, I would find furniture covered up, books and cutlery in boxes, everything ready to be shipped out.

I hug both of them—my eighteen-year-old son and sixteen-year-old daughter—and then we sit back down on the floor, as if waiting for the movers. No one is saying anything.

After about thirty minutes, my son's Twitter feed begins spitting out facts—scores arrested, a sting operation—and, a few thumb swipes later, the savvy teenager somehow finds the official government complaint document online. The three of us gather around his phone as he reads the incoming tweets and clicks around the complaint. I've left my glasses at home, so I rely on him to relay the news as he finds it.

"She's mentioned in the complaint." Pause.

"Not till page fifteen, though." Pause.

"She's charged with 'honest services' something. Maybe she was a witness." Pause, as he reads on. Then, suddenly, both he and his sister gasp.

"What?" I cry out. "What did you read?"

"It's the transcript," he says. "Of her conversations with Rick Singer. She paid Rick Singer to have someone else take my ACT for me."

Watching my son discover that his accomplishments are not his own—after all the pride he had shown months earlier in sharing his ACT score with me, with his friends, with my mom—guts me. Goodness knows what it does to him. I cry every time I relive that moment. Over the coming weeks, each implication of that one sentence will occur to each of us differently, and at different times, each new day bringing a new shard of pain, but at that moment every bit of it hits us all at once. My daughter takes herself away to the living room and crumples on the couch, while my son and I just stand there. I hug him.

"What's going to happen now, Dad?"

I hug him closer. I find myself reassuring him, that his mom will be fine, that we'll sort this out, that his life is not over. He looks at me and walks away into the sanctuary of his bedroom.

The truth is, I can't be sure of any of those things. I'm doing all I can to keep it together for him. A helpless feeling. Around and around in my head, the questions: How will the world ever come to see him for who he really is? How could I have let this happen to him? How can I pull him through?

I want to tell the world that my son's defining quality is his loyalty; that he is a stickler for rules; that from five years old he wouldn't let me pull down the window shade next to our airplane seat because that shade just might belong to the seat in front of us; that he hates the limelight; that he is not a type-A striver; that his friends count on him to have their backs; that what I am proudest of is that so many of them asked him to stand up and speak for them at their confirmations or bar mitzvahs.

I want the world to know all of this about him. But standing there that morning in the hallway, I see the years stretching away, with him getting smaller and smaller, disappearing under the weight of the scandal. I find I cannot breathe.

Kids are surprisingly resilient though, aren't they. It's six months later. He and I are sitting in an auditorium with about fifty freshmen at the school that accepted him based on his first and valid ACT result. It's orientation. The students and their parents, or in his case, him and me. The alarmingly peppy leader onstage asks each student to think of one thing to share with everyone else, something surprising, something you might be proud of, or not—*something that'll help us know you a little better.*

I sit there, paralyzed. What's he going to share? That very morning the new *Vanity Fair* issue has come out with his mother on the cover alongside Felicity Huffman and Lori Loughlin. As I wrack my brains, thinking of how I can intercede for him, maybe write a couple of suggestions on a scrap of paper and slide it over to him, suddenly it's his turn. I straighten my back, survey the room with defiance, wait for the inevitable.

After introducing himself, he said, "I'm from Los Angeles. And what you might not know about me is . . . that I can bite my toenails. Not that I do it all the time. Just that I can."

The room giggles. No one challenges him. No one sneers. He didn't need me and my defiance. I sit back in my seat, and comfort myself with the knowledge that he will gradually find his way through this. He will find his voice.

All about the Brand

Our kids' resilience doesn't absolve us, though. The educational ecosystem we've built creates stress for our children—and parents—and fails to prepare them to contribute their best at work. It is time, now, to start to dismantle it, and gradually reassemble it into something centered on each child.

To do this, we'll have to do two things: First, reveal what our schools are currently doing to hurt us so much, and pinpoint which practices must be removed from our schools for good. And second, in parallel, create a blueprint for a better system, something that all of us can rally behind and on which each of us can take action.

So, to begin, let's just be clear and say that, yes, there are millions of brilliant and well-intended teachers in the world. You've been blessed with some, and so have I. I would not be the person I am without Mrs. Whitehouse's passion for great literature, Mr. Hetherington's dogged faith in my ability to learn Latin. These outstanding teachers are doing their level best to help each one of us learn and grow.

And yet they are doing so, in many cases, in spite of rather than because of our educational ecosystem.

To build a better system—for them and for us—we'll need to start by answering this fundamental question: What is school for?

At the most basic level, school is for childcare. It was designed by the Germans in the mid-nineteenth century so that parents could be freed up to leave the house, and the children within it, and venture out to the factories and offices that were just springing up and that needed the physical presence of working adults. The industrial revolution took labor outside of the home for the first time, and so it required a system set up at scale to give parents the confidence to leave their kids for ten to twelve hours a day. School was that system. School was, and is, for childcare so that we parents are freed up to contribute economic output. School lets us go to work.

Of course, school did originally have a second purpose: namely, to educate the children so that they could grow up to add their own labor to the economy. Thus children were taught to read and write and do elementary mathematics, and then they were split into those who would go into the trades—these kids were moved quickly into practical apprenticeships—and those who would go into professional services, such as lawyers, doctors, engineers, financiers, and businessmen. This latter group was kept in school and taught how to think by exposing them to great works of literature, history, and philosophy.

This worked quite well for decades. An increasingly literate population could participate more in the country's growing economy. They would not only know how to add their productivity to the country's GDP, but also become much more prolific and educated consumers. Literate people bought more.

Today, as odd as it is to say, the importance of this purpose has diminished. Yes, it still makes sense to teach our children how to read and write, but beyond that, fewer and fewer of the skills and facts they're being taught at school will help them excel in their chosen professions. Why? First, because the jobs they will be getting in ten years' time when they graduate haven't even been invented yet, so it's impossible for school to be preparing them for these jobs. And second, because even those jobs that appear to be perennials, such as nursing, or auto construction and repair, or selling, or hospitality, are changing at such a rapid pace that companies' greatest challenge is reskilling their current workers.

So, if this purpose has been outpaced by the speed of change in today's working world, if school is no longer for preparing the students for their future careers, then what is it for? Why do we devote so much time and energy and money to it, and invest so much of our own parental prestige in how our kids perform in this thing called school? Why the proliferation of Facebook mummy and daddy groups, why the extreme professionalization of youth sports, why the billions spent on tutors and test prep, why the parents willing to shred their reputations and break the law in order to get their kids to succeed in this thing called school? What is school for that it can dominate us and ruin us, financially and morally, for decades?

The most banal of answers is this: school is for sorting. For sorting students into categories and levels of proficiency. You go this way, you go that way. You jump up here, you stay down there.

Who wants this sorting? The working world does. The working world's companies and organizations are the customers of schools and colleges. They are what colleges and schools serve. They are the ones who use the "product"—the graduating students. They are the ones with the money—in the form of salaries, donations, and investments. They demand this sorting of students not least because it makes it easier to know where to go to recruit the right kind of employee. And so these organizations put big-time pressure on the colleges to presort each student so it's clear which sort of student they can expect from each college.

Under pressure from the working world, colleges double down on their sorting mission. They have realized that each college must crystalize its brand, as in "which sorts of students we will produce for you." In education, branding functions in exactly the same way it does in business: namely, differentiating products that, on their face, seem exactly the same.

What's the difference in functionality between a Samsung phone and an iPhone? Nothing, except that Apple's brand carries stronger positive associations than Samsung's brand. What's the difference between a Tesla Model 3 and a Polestar? In terms of mechanics, range, and safety, basically nothing. The only difference is the brand—Elon Musk, Tesla's CEO, is omnipresent, and you know exactly what he and his company stands for. Polestar, as yet, has zero brand credibility, and its sales will suffer until it fixes this. It doesn't need to share the same brand as Tesla, it just needs to identify and then amplify a brand of its own.

Colleges work the same way. An engineering student graduating from MIT is exactly the same as an engineering student graduating from Cal Poly or Emory or the University of Vermont, and they know how to do exactly the same things. The board of trustees of MIT does not like this state of affairs, and so it tries to do everything it can to ensure that the brand of MIT stands for something memorable and specific. If MIT is going to continue to secure the tuition funding, the attention of the working world, and the alumni donations to its general endowment fund, then it must ensure that the letters "MIT" stand for a brand, in the same way that "Tesla" stands for a brand.

It's not just MIT. Every well-run college knows that its purpose is to communicate to the working world what its brand is—*what sort of students we produce here*—and it must make every decision so as to reinforce its desired brand characteristics.

And look, there is nothing wrong with this fixation on brand. Every single organization needs to find a way to differentiate itself, and colleges are no exception. They *should* take their brand seriously.

The damage occurs because they've chosen to use our children as the raw material for their brand building blocks. It's a branding ecosystem, a marketing machine in which the child is the mechanism, not the purpose. *Their brand* is the purpose. And this ecosystem is perceived to be so powerful, so real, so deterministic that if a child starts off with the wrong brand—the thinking goes—then they are unlikely ever to break themselves free and rebrand themselves.

This is why some parents contort themselves into such desperate displays in order to get their kid into the right kindergarten. Put them in a Tesla, and they are made for life. But let them climb into a Polestar, and they're disadvantaged from the get-go.

Data for the Brand

Look at schools through this sorting/branding lens, and the point of all kinds of strange rituals suddenly becomes clear. Why is Cal Poly sending Myshel's son a recruiting brochure?

And why is Myshel leaving it out on the kitchen island in hopes that he will see its headline, "YOU belong with us!" and pick it up and read it?

She leaves it there because she genuinely believes that Cal Poly might want him, and that if she can lure him into being interested in it, then she might have helped him climb into a Tesla.

But, of course, Cal Poly doesn't want him. Well, it might, but it didn't send the brochure to him for this reason. Nor did the hundred other colleges send their brochures for this reason. They want a low admissions percentage. Because this helps their brands. The more students who apply, the lower their admissions percentages will be, and the more they'll be able to build their brands around how selective they are. They made these glossy brochures with images of leafy autumnal quads, and strolling, smiling students, each one more enticing than the next, promising that *You are right for us, you belong with us*, because then he will—maybe—apply to them, which will drive up their applicant numbers, drive down their acceptance rates, and thereby drive up their brand value.

Cal Poly will then release its acceptance rate to the US News and World Report college rankings list in hopes that this year the school will rise just a couple of spots. Go to the website, and you'll see that acceptance rate is the very first piece of information the report offers you on Cal Poly—or any college. Last year, as it happens, Cal Poly's acceptance rate was 30 percent, which US News and World Report was pleased to compare with that of UC Davis (41 percent) and UC Santa Barbara (32 percent).

This rankings list has great power over you and your kids. You may not be aware of this, but many college boards of trustees connect bonus levels for the college president and administrators to where the college lands on the US News and World Report list. Some colleges—think Ivy League, Stanford, Oxbridge—consider themselves above the demands of this list, but virtually every other college is acutely aware that this list functions as a brand monitor, precisely calibrating the relative brand strength of each institution.

Sure, anyone who knows anything about data knows that US News and World Report and the data underpinning it are hopelessly unreliable—guesswork masquerading as precision—but not only does it grab eyeballs, it also determines people's bonuses.

So yes, colleges will do everything they can to generate as many applications as they can, knowing that they will accept very few, because then they might rise a couple of spots on the list, the working world will pay them more heed, the alumni will pay them more money, and they'll be able to build that new library, or aquatics center, or rose garden.

And you know what else would add precision to their brand? If the high schools could find some way to quantify the academic prowess of their students. Hence the building of a grade point average system. Administered by high schools and then provided to colleges, GPA enables colleges to compare each student, to select only those with a certain GPA or

above, and then to publicize the average GPA of their incoming freshman class.

This need to add precision to a brand also explains the
existence of standardized general intelligence tests such as
the SAT and the ACT. The research reveals that there is actually no such thing as general intelligence and that these tests
do not predict anything in the real world, whether earning
power, happiness, life span, or well-being. But the colleges
aren't using them for this reason. All they really want any of
these tests to do is to have some predictive relationship to
college GPA. This way, they can announce to the world that
they—the colleges—have an average SAT/ACT score for their
incoming freshman class of X, and that, as a result, they can
anchor their college brand as one that will produce for you—
dear working world—college graduates with an average college GPA of Y.

Yes, colleges know that GPA shows zero predictive relationship to subsequent earning power or happiness or well-
being in real life, but, again, that's not really their concern.
Their concern is to present to the working world a coherent
brand, and so their ability both to select their students based
on SAT/ACT score and to publicize GPAs is paramount.

The fact that all these tests lead to the need for tutors
and special test prep programs—all of which cost money—
and that therefore their branding needs are tilting the floor
ever more toward the most affluent parents, is regrettable,
but, again, not really their concern. They are just defining the

criteria for their student sorting process. If certain parents choose to spend thousands to help their kids meet these criteria, well, that's their choice.

As a student, if you've ever wondered why this fixation with grades, why this need to suffer through or pay for SAT/ACT tutoring, why this arms race of college application creation, why am I putting myself through this, why does this feel like such a battle, why does this feel like I'm part of something that has nothing to do with me, an ecosystem that doesn't care about me or understand me or even see me—good question. Middle school, high school, and college have not been designed to grow you. You and your beautiful uniqueness are almost irrelevant to the needs of the educational ecosystem you entered after kindergarten.

Take the stamps—magna cum laude, summa cum laude. How happy is the institution to brand you with these stamps—yet another source of branding data—and how damaging they can be for the individual student. When Myshel made magna cum laude, she got an honors cord, which she proudly wore at graduation. She worked so hard for that cord. She overscheduled herself, gave up eating, pulled all-nighters to complete assignments, amped herself up on amphetamines to stay alert in class, and hoped, above all, that her mom would see the cord and be so very proud.

In the real world, of course, her mom wasn't proud. She was distraught. Her mom looked at her seventy-four-pound frame and crumpled. Stamps such as magna cum laude are like a medal bestowed on a young soldier by a general to distract the soldier from what's really going on. While Myshel was striving for her stamp, what got lost was who Myshel really is. All the interesting things about her—what she loves, what piques her attention, when and how she learns best, what sparks her creativity, what shuts her down—all the stuff that would give her self-efficacy in the working world, and, frankly, that the working world should dearly love to know about her, all of that is hidden by the striving for the stamp. The stamp serves only the college, as the medal serves only the general.

And how about the GPA? As a parent, you get on your child every single week to maintain their GPA. You make them take extra AP classes to inflate their GPA. You stress out their teenage years and sour their social development so that they can preserve their GPA. They need this GPA, you tell them, so they can get into the right college.

But what is this GPA? From a data standpoint, it's a mess. Have you heard of a thing called inter-rater reliability (IRR)? It sounds obscure, but for you and your child it's a very meaningful concept. IRR refers to two raters' ability to grade the same test in exactly the same way. If you give your child's essay to one teacher and they grade it, and then you give it to another teacher and they grade it, do these two teachers arrive at the same grade? If they do, all is good. You have 100 percent IRR. But if they don't, then your child's grade is merely made up—unreliable data.

Some subjects have, on average, higher than 90 percent IRR: math, physics, some parts of biology, and chemistry.

Other subjects—in fact, most other subjects—languish below the 50 percent level. English, the parts of history that don't involve memorizing dates, social studies, a foreign language, they all have less than 50 percent IRR.

Imagine that.

This means that a student's GPA data changes significantly depending on which teacher is grading which paper. In the UK, researchers examined just how much. What they found was that in subjects where the IRR sank below 50 percent, more than one-quarter of all students would have seen their grades drop or rise one spot with another teacher—an A to a B, or a B to an A. And as a result, many of these students would have gotten accepted into very different colleges.

Which means that your child's GPA is junk data. By telling our children it's not junk, we're messing them up. They know how important reliable data is—leveling up in video games is often based on reliable data, as is social network data—and yet we, almost from the get-go, tell them that the data that defines them and their future is reliable when it isn't.

A GPA of 3.69—a data point that colleges will receive and will wind up publishing in order to define their brand—isn't real data. It is designed and built so that high schools can service their customers, the colleges. But it's not reliable. It's not valid. And it reveals so very little about the child.

A Love + Work School Curriculum

If all this was an overstatement, if schools and colleges were genuinely interested in who each student is, then here's what we should see:

- We should see classes and curricula focused on the student's identity. Classes that help the student figure out how much of their identity is tied to characteristics they share with others, such as gender, religion, or nationality, and how much is connected to the uniqueness of their personality.

- There would be classes on how to use the raw material of a regular week of school to figure out what they truly love, or how they learn best, or when they are deeply in their element, or how they build the healthiest relationships. Not classes about a *theory* of learning, or creativity, or relationships, but about how *you*—this one beautiful, unique human—learn, or create, or build relationships.

- We should see classes that help the student cut through the complex social pressures of their teenage years to identify their own distinct voice, and then guide this student in how to cultivate their voice into something valuable for others.

- And while this student is learning about their idiosyncrasies and how to contribute them, they would also be learning about how to honor the idiosyncrasies of others. These classes would help the student demystify the apparent paradox of the need for racial and gender equality, with the fact that no gender or race is monolithic—there are more differences within gender, or within race, than between genders, and between races. These classes would help the student spot the clues to other people's uniqueness, and would counsel the student on how to be a supporter, an ally, an amplifier of the uniqueness of others.

• There would be classes on how to make decisions, how to build resilience, how to join a new team, how to be on multiple teams, how to explain yourself to your new team members, how to talk about your strengths without bragging, how to talk about your loves without sounding self-involved.

We would see a decade-long curriculum all focused on how this student can develop mastery in what they love and how they can contribute these loves to others. Companies would benefit hugely from students learning in these sorts of classes—they'd be able to hire new recruits with much more self-confidence, self-efficacy, personal resilience, generosity, and ability to quickly collaborate with others.

But, more importantly, think about how these classes would benefit students. Learning about themselves, the galaxies that they and they alone contain, the responsibility that comes from this power, the assurance that emanates from this power—what a gift this would be to all those extraordinarily unique individuals who entrust themselves to our care.

If we were truly worried about the psychological health and development of each student, these are the kinds of classes we would see.

At present we don't see any of them.

Occasionally, a college will have its students take Strengths-Finder or Myers-Briggs or some other assessment, but these are fun distractions—helium balloons at a birthday party. They are not part of a decade-long commitment to help each student develop mastery in themselves.

There is a better way. It can be a lot to think about because you don't want to mess up your kids; in fact, you want to do the opposite. You want to help your kids thrive, and this ecosystem of schools and colleges is so powerful and so persuasive. But there is a way to push back, to pull down Oz's branding curtain, as it were, and set your children and yourself up for a very different kind of education.

It's not right to say that we are part of the problem. We are the *entire* problem, and only if we—all of us—make specific changes to this ecosystem will we start to do right by our kids.

A Love + Work School Manifesto

Here is a top ten list of changes for our kids. It serves as a manifesto for child-centered schools and colleges—presented in ascending order of difficulty. This list is not meant to be exhaustive. But rather, I offer it as a way to stimulate your own thinking about what actions *you* can take—as a student or a teacher or a parent—right now.

1. Stop Seeing Parenting as a Competitive Sport

We keep score with each test taken, each club joined, each summer program attended, each charity volunteered for, and the college acceptance serves as the finish line. In truth, parenting as a competitive sport has no finish line and no winners, only losers, most of them children.

2. Stop Projecting Your Own Fears onto Your Children

Some say that the parents who participated in the college cheating scandal did so because they were entitled. Maybe some did feel this way. But what rings truer to me is that they participated because they were frightened.

Know someone's fear and you'll know their need. Know their need and you'll understand their behavior. These parents were frightened for their kids' future, and so they *needed* to do something, anything, even cheating and lying, to make that future more secure. And in so doing, they not only committed themselves to a lifetime of lying to their kids, they also spread the deeper lie that fear is bad and any action that reduces it is justified.

The truth, of course, is that fear of the future is a sensible and adaptive part of the human condition. The challenge of life is not to reduce fear, but rather to feel it, understand it, and move through it. To admit your fears, to even love them, and yet to still act, to risk and fall and rise to risk again, this is the sign of health.

When we strive to reduce fear, we wind up fortifying fear, and weakening children.

3. Stop Reading the US News and World Report College Rankings

And demand that boards of trustees uncouple bonuses from a college's placement on the list.

When we think about how to make change in the world, where is our biggest source of power and control? We have so much power in what we buy and consume. Why don't we come together as a parent team? Doesn't matter if you have a three-year-old or a sixteen-year-old. What we consume tells society what we deem important. If we stop buying, they stop making. These rankings were put together in order to sell subscriptions and advertising, but now they wield such power that colleges contort themselves to move up a couple of spots, and parents pressure their kids to apply to only the "best" colleges.

The truth is that the data underpinning these rankings is arcane, unreliable, and falsely precise, all noise, no signal, signifying nothing.

But it does make good copy. We are sacrificing our children on the altar of the US News and World Report rankings. Stop reading it.

4. Start Reading the Research

Which college you go to predicts virtually nothing about your subsequent success, and absolutely nothing about your psychological well-being.

The research is ongoing, of course, and all findings are provisional, but thus far two findings stand out: first, which college you attend does a poor job of predicting your earning potential and your long-term physical and psychological health.

And second, the demographic that is most helped by Ivy League attendance is minority students—a finding best explained by the fact that their college experience exposes them to new and powerful networks.

This makes a strong case for continuing with affirmative action to offer places to students with less socioeconomic advantage and to promote more diverse student bodies. It also reveals that any comfortably well-off, middle-class Caucasian parent who stresses out their child, or cheats on tests for their child, in order to push her into a "better" school is wasting their time. The "better" school won't better her.

5. Start Pressuring Colleges to Get Rid of Standardized Tests

What precisely do the ACT and SAT scores predict later in life? Precisely nothing. They are a score on an arbitrary list of questions, and, as with the arbitrary list of questions on the IQ test, they are valid only as measures of a child's ability to answer the questions that some test maker decided to include in the test.

Yes, there is a great deal of money to be made in the constructing and selling of these tests, but as a tool to reveal the uniqueness of a child's mind, they are utterly useless.

Did I pay for my son's test prep to ensure he was ready for the tests I find so useless? Yes. He studied and was tutored in the hope of a good grade, and he did get a good grade on his first and true attempt at the test. Was it the "right" score? Who cares. What's more important is that there are millions of other kids who cannot afford the test prep. What do we do about them? Infuse tutoring into scholarships? Or maybe tax the tests and use that tax to fund government-run tutoring programs?

A better solution is to just get rid of the tests. Both of them, the SAT and the ACT, are the worst sort of pseudoscience. Many schools are beginning to move away from them, thank goodness. Let's add speed to that retreat, throw our parental weight behind it.

And instead let's rely on high school transcripts, personal essays, and interviews. Yes, these take longer both to acquire and to sift through, and offer little in the way of shortcuts, but sorry, college admissions departments, that's precisely the point. We don't want to sacrifice the vivid uniqueness of our children just so you can save some time in your admissions process. Just ask our children to submit their high school transcripts, to write essays describing themselves and their passions, and conduct actual interviews with them. Then make a qualitative decision based on what you've seen in each child. Nothing wrong with you using your judgment to make a qualitative decision. Far better than relying on the shortcut of fake data.

6. Start Banning the Use of Clubs, Activities, or Charity Work on College Applications

The listing of these activities was begun, presumably, to allow the child to present the full extent of who she really is, but they no longer serve that purpose.

They have become badges, applicant "flair" that she is coerced to pin to her application. Thus displayed, they favor the wealthy, as each one incurs a cost—the more esoteric, the greater the cost. If you are a nurse supervisor getting off your late-night shift, do you have the time or the energy or the money to sign your daughter up for that perfect volunteer project?

Even more alarming, these "badges" mask who the applicant truly is. Did the student really so love fencing, or coxswaining, or yearbook editing that he couldn't imagine a world without it, or were these "loves" an artifact of his need to pretty up his application?

Let's stop covering up our kids with badges. If they have a hobby or a special interest, have them write about it in their essay or describe it with passion in their interview.

7. Start Pressuring Middle Schools and High Schools to Develop Self-Mastery Curricula

These classes and courses should focus on three areas: 1) How each child can, over time and through their regular life at home and school, identify the loves and strengths that make them unique, 2) How each child can find ways to turn these strengths into contribution, loves into work, and 3) How each student can use their understanding of their loves and those of others to join and build highly collaborative teams.

The working world would fall over itself to support the development of this curricula. According to the ADP Research Institute's most recent global study, 85 percent of all work is done on teams, so if schools actually made it a priority to teach a student how to know in detail what they bring to each team, and how to offer these loves in the most productive way, then the working world would cheer from the rooftops.

More importantly, though, each student will develop far greater self-assurance and confidence if we teach them that learning is less about acquiring and being tested on outside knowledge, and more about developing and contributing the uniqueness already present inside them.

The fact that no such curricula currently exist is both a huge productivity miss and a moral failing. Demand curricula change.

8. Invert the Classroom

Currently, the generally accepted method of teaching is to impart information in the classroom and then have the child do homework and assignments on their own. This makes sense only if the goal of middle and high school is to use each student to generate quiz, test, and assignment scores that can then be inputted into admissions forms and sent off to colleges.

But if the goal of school became to help each student identify and contribute their loves, then you would flip the classroom around. Each student would do their learning and reading by themselves at home, and then in the classroom the teacher would help each student refine their unique way of turning the new information, facts, or processes into actual work. Each student's way of doing this—of solving a math problem, writing a paper, learning a language—is idiosyncratic. The classroom should be the place where the teacher pays attention to this idiosyncrasy.

Teaching thus will cease to be solely information transfer, and will instead become coaching of the individual student. This isn't more work for teachers—with fewer assignments to grade, it will actually be less work. But in terms of helping the student grow, it will certainly be more effective work.

9. Get Rid of Grade Point Averages

From a data standpoint, they are an embarrassment. As currently calculated, a student's GPA is junk data since it is generated from many different subjects, most of which have IRR levels languishing in the low seventies and below. Which means that these data sources are, in simple terms, bad data— and, as anyone with an ounce of statistics knowledge knows, if you combine systematically bad data with good data, you render *all* the summary data bad. Bad as in "it does not measure accurately what it purports to measure."

So, all of us parents should raise our voices against the use of GPA as a measure of our students. Any school or college using GPA should be shamed by coalitions of parents. Schools and colleges use GPA because it makes their "sorting" job easier. But that doesn't make the data right. Our students deserve better.

This does not mean that we should universally ditch grades and grading—some schools have, but many have not, and from a data standpoint that's OK. To be clear: it is fine for a teacher to read a history paper and, based on their particular expert judgment, assign the paper a grade. It is not fine for the school to then turn that grade into a number, add that number to all the other grades/numbers, and produce a summary GPA number. For most subjects, the grade is not an objective measure, but is instead the subjective response of an idiosyncratic teacher. We pay the teacher for the wisdom of their response, and we expect them to know their subject well. But we should not expect them to be the perfectly objective arbiter of what is truly an A versus a B, nor should we dumb down subjects into true/false or multiple-choice questions just so that we can get every quiz to generate a perfectly objective number.

We should just ask teachers to use their best judgment in grading. We should submit all of these best judgments to colleges in the form of a transcript. And we should *never* add these subjective judgments together into a GPA as though they were objective, reliable scores. Because they aren't and never will be.

10. Make College Free

Of students who graduated in 2018, 69 percent did so burdened with, on average, $29,000 in debt. Looking back across all previous graduating classes, we now have forty-five million citizens still carrying student loan debt, for a total of $1.65 trillion owed. Putting aside for a moment the macroeconomic inefficiency of tying people up in twice as much student loan debt as they have credit card debt, think about what this does to the psychological well-being of each graduate.

When the average monthly student loan payment is $393, a graduate makes their first steps toward contribution to society guided not by passion, or mission, or self-discovery, but by financial pressure: Will this job be able to pay down my debt? How many quality teachers or nurses do we lose because those instinctively drawn to these professions do the math and discover the money doesn't add up? Flipping this around, how many people choose lucrative roles such as law-yering or doctoring that don't fit their authentic selves, simply because finances trump fit? How many dreams are destroyed by the weight of debt?

It's hard to put exact numbers to these questions, but as I shared earlier, we do know that only 14 percent of people feel that their job gives them a chance to do their best work every day; that nurses have levels of PTSD twice as high as veter-ans returning from war zones; that respect for the teaching profession is lower than it's ever been; that 73 percent of phy-sicians would not tell their children to follow them into med-icine, and that as a result, by 2025 here in the US we'll have a shortage of twenty thousand doctors.

Not all of these data points can be explained by the pressures of student debt, but common sense tells us that something's amiss. A healthy, productive team is one where each person finds a role in which to express the very best of themselves. A healthy, productive nation requires the same. It's hard enough for each of us to find our way toward the role or roles that do indeed call on our loves; it's nigh impossible when our vision is clouded by the shroud of debt.

I have benefited from many advantages in my life, not least that I grew up a middle-class, well-educated white male in an advanced and stable economy. But my greatest advantage was that my college tuition was entirely paid for by my nation of birth. Someone, somewhere made the decision that I would be more likely to contribute more, and more intelligently, if debt didn't distract me.

Those were the good old days. For the sake of our kids, ourselves, and our nation, let's see if we can find our way back there.

OK, that's the top ten list. Taken together, it can appear daunting, so as you march forward and make your voice heard, hold on to this one insight: *The most powerful way to help your child learn and grow is to reveal to them what is already inside them, and to show them how to turn what is inside them into contribution. To turn loves into work.*

Any action, any class, any educational reform that gets you closer to this is a significant step toward doing what is right by your children.

A Love + Work School Manifesto

1. Stop seeing parenting as a competitive sport

2. Stop projecting your own fears onto your children

3. Stop reading the US News and World Report college rankings

4. Start reading the research

5. Start pressuring colleges to get rid of standardized tests

6. Start banning the use of clubs, activities, or charity work on college applications

7. Start pressuring middle schools and high schools to develop self-mastery curricula

8. Invert the classroom

9. Get rid of grade point averages

10. Make college free

Your Children Are Not Your Children

One Thing I Hope You Learned from Your Parents

When my son was five and my daughter three, we arrived at my son's best friend's birthday party only to bump into Coco the Clown schlepping his clown kit down the driveway.

"Are you done?" the kids' mother asked.

"Yes," Coco replied, "the show ended a few minutes ago."

We were late. The kids didn't seem to mind too much—clowns were meh to my son and substandard Disney princesses to my daughter.

Their mom reached into her purse.

"If I give you this"—she held out a couple of $20 bills—"can you stay for another thirty minutes for my kids?"

"Er, sure," said Coco.

This is a particular approach to parenting. Not entitled, necessarily, but extremely proactive. You reach in and take every single step you can think of to get your kids what they just might want.

Thinking back on those years, the image I have of so many parents around me is of superstar *Pac-Man* players. They had a grip on the joystick, and as they surveyed the field of play, they could somehow see further and faster than anyone else. They would sense opportunity or danger, jerk the joystick this way and that, and their children would move safely forward, darting around corners, the danger averted. With these parents at the helm, the kids made it through, level after level, eating the fruit, munching the ghosts, racing to the next level and the next, and still with all their lives intact.

And who can fault parents for grabbing the joystick so tightly? If you don't have kids, you might not quite understand this, but all parents know the feeling that their child is as vulnerable as a heart outside the body. You can see it beating, you know you must do everything in your power to protect it, and yet there it is, completely exposed to all the abuse the world can throw at it. If it gets hurt, you will die. It is your heart.

And so it's hardly surprising that, when shown a way to control the world, a way that can protect your heart, you grab on and try to maneuver the world so that your child emerges unscathed.

In the face of this always-on joystick jerking—perhaps by disposition, perhaps as a reverse overreaction—I found myself stepping back. Not, I confess, as a result of some carefully considered parenting strategy, but more because I couldn't find my place in a world of so many furiously skilled *Pac-Man* players.

The fact that, during my daughter's first afternoon nap at home, I managed to roll her out of the Moses basket onto the brick steps in our backyard, or that I once slipped down our stairs carrying my two-year-old son and broke his leg in two places, I took to be a sign that my stepping back was sensible.

But regardless of my rationalizations, I never tried to take the joystick. I didn't find the right way to label the game unhealthy, to point out that the joystick wasn't connected to anything real, that the figures dashing through the maze weren't our kids, at least not the best versions of them. I didn't do any of these things.

In the days that followed their mom's arrest, I found myself lurching from self-recrimination for not prying the joystick loose, to shock at how quickly the world can reach in and harm my kids, and then, always, to anger. It would start small and sad, doused with tears, but then the tears would dry, I'd reread the FBI documents, trying to imagine how and why and what the hell, and the fire would rage out of control. I'd pace the bedroom at all hours of the night, banging my fists against the wall as I tried to imagine how this could have happened to my son.

And in the end, the anger spent, the self-pity done with, the traffic rumbling to life on a bright new day in LA, my only guide for how to move forward was the memory of my own mom and dad. Over the years I had rushed hither and yon—to school, to university, to a job in the US—and hadn't given their approach to parenting much thought. Now, I found my-self returning to them again and again.

I'll share with you one aspect of what they did. Not because they were perfect parents—none are.

Not because the data necessarily supports their approach—I'm not aware of any longitudinal study either supporting or contradicting what they did.

I'm sharing it simply because, when the refining fire of this intense period in my and my kids' lives had done its work, this one crystalline insight was all that remained. It will be what I take with me for all the years I have left as a parent.

I hope it helps you as much as it has me.

Graeme + Jo

My dad, Graeme, was the first in our family to attend college. He was an empiricist, grounded in the belief that, though faith had its place, the only way to move through the world was to do credible research and to trust the results, even if, at first, you don't agree with them. On his deathbed, I remember, he complained bitterly that what he called "the medical profession" knew nothing about his condition.

"Marcus, the medical profession say I've only got a few months to live, but where's their research on that? Where's their research?!"

I can still hear the outrage through his plummy home counties accent.

My mom, Jo, saw life differently. She was from tough North Yorkshire stock—three generations of coal miners—but her grandmother was a faith healer, who took people into the terraced house she shared with my mom's family, laid hands on them each morning, and then six months later the "house guest" would walk out cured. My mom inherited her faith, and her gift, and now spends her days—she's eighty going on sixty—healing the scars and souls of her patients.

So, yes, Graeme and Jo were very different, but they did share this deep-seated belief that love-making is space-making. To love your children is to see your children, and you can't see your children if you don't leave them the space to make their own choices.

They played out this belief with my younger sister and elder brother, but I felt it so intimately on account of my stammer.

The perverse thing about a stammer is not only that there's nothing anyone else can do about it, but also that the more they try, the worse it gets—the perfect metaphor for everything we do as parents.

Initially, Graeme and Jo took me to a speech pathologist to try to fix me, where I had to learn set phrases and repeat them ad infinitum—as though after the thousandth "Peter Piper picked a peck of pickled peppers" my mouth muscles would form memory, strengthen and sharpen, and I would burst through the dam.

This never happened. My mind-mouth connection would break under the pressure to perform, spasms of something other than speech would spurt from my mouth, which, upon hearing it, would scare me, stop me, and I would shut my mouth and shut down.

As all parents would be, Graeme and Jo must have been in despair to see their child suffer, and I know they would have done anything to free me of my misfiring synapses. And yet, when they saw that their interventions actually increased my disfluency, when they saw their well-intended efforts actually hurt me, they were wise and loving enough to stop.

Instead, they just let me be. They surrounded me with a bubble of love and then gave me space to bounce around within it. After the first try, they never again took me to a pathologist. Yes, they sent me to a smaller grade school than my elder brother attended, but then they left me alone to bump into my world. The love bubble would catch me if I fell and bounce me right back up again. I was a stuttering, stammering Weeble. Wobbly, but well loved.

This well-loved space they created was not just laissez-faire in parenting. It was a deliberate strategy—the sort that led to my dad sending me off to an internship in the US for the summer, telling me he would splurge for a one-way plane ticket to Chicago and a Greyhound bus pass to Nebraska, and that it was up to me, at sixteen, to figure out how to earn enough money to buy my return ticket home. They were, I now realize, inordinately comfortable with space—my elder brother and his friends cycled round France when they were fifteen; my younger sister moved to live in Munich at sixteen.

I never had the opportunity to share my realizations with Dad. He died from an "unresearched" condition on

October 31, 2017, only one day after we shared a Scotch in his little flat.

I wish I could now look straight into those stern, soft blue eyes and say, "Thank you, Dad. I am only able to do the work that I do today, work that I so hope benefits the world, because of the space you gave, that one-way Greyhound bus ticket." I wish I could rewind the tape and share with him what happened that morning when my stammer went away.

On the day itself I kept what happened to myself; didn't want to jinx it by naming it. Though by that time I had figured out how to limit the damage of my stammer—keep conversations short, never try to tell a joke because the stammer will kill the punch line, avoid introducing myself to people—it was still the dominant force in my life. The night before the chapel reading I wrote about in chapter 8, I walked into the dark, cold chapel with my headmaster, Mr. Pratt, and he attempted to coax me through the piece. The place was empty, the glossy wood of the pews reflecting the candle light back to me as I stood at the lectern and tried to cajole the words out. They stuttered out unbalanced, one staccato moment bumping into another, each phase freakishly elongated.

I held in my tears and my anger while explaining all this to Graeme and Jo over dinner. I didn't say it, but I thought and hoped that one of them would take up my cause, and reach out, and fix it, and call Mr. Pratt and tell him to not humiliate their son in this way. I mean, who wouldn't do that? What parent wouldn't call up the school and do everything in their power to stop the pain and suffering of their child?

Certainly all those *Pac-Man* parents would.

How I wished for one of those that evening.

But no, my parents weren't *Pac-Man* players. Jo didn't pick up the phone. What she did was say: "That's just lovely, Poppet, what fun that will be!" Poppet, Flugelhorn, Sausage—all loving pet names from Mom. I didn't eat a thing and barely slept the night.

The next morning, cycling the three miles to school, I pedaled extra hard, thinking that if I was exhausted from the ride I might trick my mind into being too tired to stammer. Once at school, I watched all the students walk up the hill and file in as usual. I took my place in the choir next to my friends. The chaplain began the service, and I waited for the inevitable.

And then the inevitable turned out not to be. The faces of the many sparked something in my brain, my synapses fired as they should, and my disfluency vanished. I felt the energy of the eyes staring at me, their attention was my unlocking, and I was cured.

How could Graeme and Jo have predicted all this? How could they have maneuvered me into a scenario where a stammerer's greatest fear became his greatest unlock?

Well, they couldn't. And they knew they couldn't. Instead, though they couldn't possibly have predicted it that June morning, they had proceeded nonetheless with their love-bubble space-making approach to parenting. They were smart enough to know the power of space and love, but also know that, inside this space, they knew virtually nothing.

It all sounds so predictable, even clichéd, forty years on, but can you imagine what Graeme and Jo must have been thinking that morning? Every parental instinct must have been pulling them toward that phone and yet they knew that, though calling the headmaster would serve them, it would not serve me. They didn't know what would happen that morning, but they did know that reaching in to fix it for me would limit the space in my world, and that a world with less space was, for me, a lesser world.

Looking back, I am astounded at their resolve. I get panicked to think of what would have happened if they had given in to the temptation to make the call. I wouldn't have had to speak in chapel. And so I wouldn't have stood up there and seen all those faces. I wouldn't have felt what I felt. I wouldn't have learned what I learned. And today I might not be doing what I am doing.

Such was the strength of their love for me. They put their own fears aside, and allowed me all the space I needed to act, to choose, to learn, and to strengthen my agency in the world. I was the beneficiary of two parents who had long ago released the joystick and realized that choice—my choice—is the fuel for learning.

In his poem "On Children," Kahlil Gibran writes this:

> *Your children are not your children.*
> *They are sons and daughters of Life's longing for itself.*
> *They come through you but not from you,*
> *And though they are with you yet they belong not to you.*

You are the bows from which your children as living
arrows are sent forth.
The archer sees the mark upon the path of the infinite,
and He bends you with His might that His arrows
may go swift and far.
Let your bending in the archer's hand be for gladness;
For even as He loves the arrow that flies, so He also
loves the bow that is stable.[1]

My children are not my children. Yours are not yours. We are parents, and so we are the bow, drawing our children close to us, only to then let them fly far on their own. Our role is not to direct the arrow in flight, nor to catch it when it falls, but is merely to be stable, to draw back our bowstring, and let the arrow fly into the space ahead.

Graeme and Jo allowed me this space. If you want to truly see your children, you can do the same for your kids. You can become the most intelligent, the most resolved, the most loving space-maker.

I hope that you stop looking at yourself—your parental fears and ambitions—and start seeing your kids. My son is not my daughter and never will be. His humor is dry, hers joyous. He shies away from the limelight, whereas she comes alive in its glare. Self-deprecation is his charm, while hers is exuberance. Both are loyal to a fault, both are each other's first call in times of stress, but only one of them loves to travel, while the other detests it.

Faced with this weird combination of loves and loathes, my only job as a parent is to see each for who they are, and to help them channel their loves intelligently, morally, and, in the end, productively.

Our kids, they show us who they are every day, with their thousands upon thousands of reactions, interactions, choices, and outcomes. And yet, apparently, many of us parents do not see them. We cover them in shiny tinfoil to protect them from the world, and then, when we look at them all wrapped up in foil, all we see is ourselves reflected back.

They don't need the tinfoil. They don't need the protection. They need to be seen.

As do we all.

Epilogue: Over to You

At my college they made you put on a cap and gown and then parade down the town's main street—called King's Parade—to the courthouse. Here your final exam results would be posted on the wall for the world to see whether you graduated, and if you did, how well you did. If you failed, there would be an S by your name. S stood for Special. It meant you weren't. Typical British understatement.

And then, if you passed—I did, thank goodness—you and your muckers would run, run, run to the punt place, where you'd rent a punt for the afternoon, grab your picnic provisions, and punt your way up the River Cam to a small village of watery English fields and hedgerows called Grantchester.

That day, seven of us jumped into our punt and eased our way up the Cam, but we never got to Grantchester. We went slow, all of us just beginning to realize that as close as we were that day, soon we would all scatter. The safety and certainty we all felt with one another would soon be replaced with the stresses of the unseeing masses.

The punt slid slowly up the river. Kieran was at the helm—best punter ever, best juggler too, as it happens—but this time he took us too close to the bank. The trees stood strong as we passed by underneath. We all ducked the branches, laughing, clinging to the bread and cheese and warm English beer bottles. We hit the bank. I stood up, plimsolls sloshing in the bottom of the punt. My feet now gripping the edge of the punt, I pushed the dense curtain of weeping willow branches aside, and stepped right into Lincoln's Greyhound bus terminal. One hundred one degrees Fahrenheit. Nebraska. Gallup. New people. New life.

Endings. They scare me. I don't quite know why, but they do. In every book I write or every speech I craft, I get stuck at the end.

Endings feel final. Maybe I don't like final. Of course, for the bad things I'm good with endings. But who wants to end something they love?

I loved writing this book for you.

Anyhow, here's the end.

In 2006 I made a movie. Actually, Tom Rinks made it and I just babbled on about strengths and data. Oprah saw it. Tom's the reason I was on her show. Tom was the founder and CEO of Sun Bum. America's favorite sunscreen. That part has nothing to do with the story.

You might have seen the movie. You might even have used it as the foundation of strengths-based learning in your organization.

It was the story of a boy who faces a struggle we all face: he plays the trombone in the school band, for a bandleader he loves, but deep down what he really loves to do is play the timpani. So does he follow what he loves, and leave his bandleader in the lurch with no trombonist? Or does he stifle his love and conform to what everyone else wants him to do?

About halfway through the film, we see how he's squared the circle. We see him scribbling on page after page in big blue marker. We can't see what he's writing, but we can see his joy that he's figured something out. Then we cut to him sticking something on the back of the seats of his school bus, then on locker after locker, and then finally the camera finds one of these posters and zooms in. It's just a blank sheet of paper on which he'd written "Trombone Player Wanted."

"And there's your title," said Tom.

I loved the making of that film. Writing the script with Tom. Casting the parts. Finding our lead kid. Renting out the entire Walt Disney Concert Hall for five days and shooting in that womb of an auditorium.

My favorite moment though wasn't the writing or the shooting. It was in the editing room. The very last shot. Right at the very final moment of filming, our lead had made a mistake. He accidentally looked straight into the camera.

Tom and I are watching the footage. The take was so perfect until that moment.

"Bollocks, we need to cut that. He broke the fourth wall," I say.

"Are you kidding? This is a brilliant mistake." Tom rewinds. "Watch. Look at the way he stares into the camera. I'm cutting everything after this and we're ending this thing right here."

"Wait, wha?" I was confused. This was not the plan. I'm a scientist. I needed more data.

"Look." He rewinds for the sixth time. "His eyes. They are saying, 'Over to you.'"

I wish I could insert that part of the film for you to see—by now I bet you can find it on YouTube. It's the very last frame of the very last chapter of the film. His eyes were saying exactly that. We couldn't have directed it more perfectly. He is handing it over to the viewer as if to say, "Take this, all of it, and do something with it."

Well, we are at that part of the book together. I'm looking at you. Right at you, saying, "Over to you."

This book has been all about you and how you can make sense of yourself and build a relationship with yourself based on love. I hope that has a huge benefit for you and how you choose to live your life.

Counterintuitively, though, one of the biggest changes you can make in the world is how you choose to see and understand others. The philosopher Jean-Paul Sartre, in his play *No Exit*, famously wrote that "Hell is other people." By which he meant that other people are hellish because they are not you. Their motives, their intentions, and their interests are not yours. They get in the way of yours. They misunderstand you, misrepresent you, mislead you. Hell is other people.

What I hope this book has done for you is turn this upside-down. Other people are scary only because you don't know them. But if these other people are like you—and they are—then they too have galaxies within them. They too have beautiful and intricate and unexpected patterns of loves and loathes. They too are different from anyone else of their country, their race, their gender, or even their own families. They too are a category of one.

Recent research into happiness reveals that of all the skills related to it, awe is the most highly correlated. Cultivate the skill of feeling awe—in the breathtaking expanse of a Midwestern sky at night, in the whorls and patterns of a cactus flower—and you feel less alone, less weighted down, lifted up out of the cares of your own life, and onto a higher, happier plane.

Other people can be a source of awe for you. Each person you meet is a wondrously complex creature, someone who will always reward your curiosity. Each time you ask an open-ended question and just listen, you'll give that person the gift of being seen, and you'll give yourself a chance to bring just a little more awe into your life.

So from now on, change how you think about introductions. Each time someone comes up to you, and you stiffen slightly, and prepare yourself to go through the nod-nod-shake-shake, catch yourself. Each introduction doesn't have to be an empty ritual. It can be something momentous. Not an icebreaker, but a landing on the shore of an undiscovered country. An entry into something more, something wild, and complex, and intricate, and one-of-a-kind. Each introduction is an invitation for you to enter a whole new galaxy.

Hell is other people? No, seen through the lens of love, heaven is other people. Your lens is up to you.

Hi, I'm Marcus and it's lovely to meet you.

Notes

Chapter 1

1. Mary Hayes, Frances Chumney, and Marcus Buckingham, "17 Findings on Engagement and Resilience," ADP Research Institute, September 29, 2020, https://www.adpri.org/assets/17-findings.

Chapter 2

1. Mary Hayes, Frances Chumncy, and Marcus Buckingham, "Global Workplace Study 2020," ADP Research Institute, September 29, 2020, https://www.adpri.org/assets/global-workplace-study.

2. Kimberlé Williams Crenshaw, "Color Blindness, History, and the Law," in *The House That Race Built: Original Essays by Toni Morrison, Angela Y. Davis, Cornel West, and Others on Black Americans and Politics in America Today*, ed. Wahneema Lubiano (New York: Vintage Books, 1997), loc. 5599, Kindle.

Chapter 3

1. Rafael Wlodarski and Robin I. M. Dunbar, "The Effects of Romantic Love on Mentalizing Abilities," *Review of General Psychology* 18, no. 4 (2014): 313–321, doi:10.1037/gpr0000020; Francesco Bianchi-Demicheli, Scott Grafton, and Stephanie Cacioppo, "The Power of Love on the Human Brain," *Social Neuroscience* 1, no. 2 (2006): 90–103, 10.1080/17470910600976547.

Chapter 6

1. Tait Shanafelt et al., "Career Fit and Burnout Among Academic Faculty," *Archives of Internal Medicine* 169, no. 10 (2009): 990–992; Kristine D. Olson,

"Physician Burnout—a Leading Indicator of Health System Performance?" *Mayo Clinic Proceedings* 92, no. 11 (2017): 1608–1611.

Chapter 18

1. Mary Hayes and Marcus Buckingham, "The Definitive Series: Employee Engagement," ADP Research Institute, November 17, 2020, https://www.adpri.org/assets/the-definitive-series-employee-engagement; Mary Hayes and Marcus Buckingham, "Top 10 Conclusions: The Definitive Series on Employee Engagement," ADP Research Institute, November 17, 2020, https://www.adpri.org/assets/top-10-conclusions-the-definitive-series-on-employee-engagement; Mary Hayes and Marcus Buckingham, "Engagement Is Closely Linked to Sales Performance," infographic, ADP Research Institute, November 17, 2020, https://www.adpri.org /assets/engagement-is-closely-linked-to-sales-performance.

2. Mary Hayes, Frances Chumney, and Marcus Buckingham, "Global Workplace Study 2020," ADP Research Institute, September 29, 2020, https://www.adpri.org/assets/global-workplace-study; Mary Hayes, Frances Chumney, and Marcus Buckingham, "17 Findings on Engagement and Resilience," ADP Research Institute, September 29, 2020, https://www.adpri.org /assets/17-findings.

Chapter 20

1. Kahlil Gibran, *The Prophet* (New York: Alfred A. Knopf, 1923).

Index

Acknowledgments

We thrive only in relation to one another. We rise up and discover the best of ourselves only in response to other human beings. Everything in this book is a gift bestowed by those around me. It is only because they are.

Myshel Romans found me, and the title, and the infinite loop of energy that is *Love + Work*, and the passion to not let go until it was real and done.

My children, and Myshel's boys, show us every day how precise and powerful each person's loves truly are, and what's at stake if we can create a world in which each person's loves are honored.

My team at the ADP Research Institute is extraordinary specifically because each person contributes what they love. Kristi Pavel runs all our projects with a strange-to-behold combination of grace, efficiency, relentlessness, and responsibility.

Dr. Mary Hayes is, well, there's only one Mary Hayes. Her intellectual prowess is matched only by her eventful life and her dedication to do it right.

Meredith Bohling is some uncategorizable combination of wit, insight, pragmatism, and get-it-done-ness.

Dr. Nela Richardson runs the other half of the Institute, and her perspectives on the broader economic world and our place within it have shaped my own and always will. I am so proud to be her partner.

Dr. Frances Chumney has brought her passion for precision and the rigor of deep science to all that we do.

The way Jennifer Beverage gets inside other people's minds should be illegal. Fortunately, she uses her gift only for good: for crystallizing an idea, turning it into a sequence of actions, and so building an experience that can actually change people's lives.

Kate Fay is our musician in the corporate world, always looking for meaning and melody.

Jo, Mum, thank you for seeing the good in us all and for showing me what lifelong love really looks like.

Pippa, no words really. Thank you for the inspiration. And the love. And the talking. And the being there.

Neil, your march through life is love filled and beautiful and destined, even on those days when it feels like none of those things.

And to the team at Harvard Business Review Press: my editor, Jeff Kehoe, I really don't know how you do it, but you have a way of seeing a project so clearly, and holding tightly to what you see, while still allowing it to live in a very messy space for a very long time. Julie Devoll, you are the call we all always want to take, because the ideas will be on point and the possibilities front-loaded. Jen Waring, Stephani Finks, Felicia Sinusas, Erika Heilman, and, of course, Adi Ignatius, thank you for taking this project's smallest details and its grandest ambitions so seriously.

About the Author

Marcus Buckingham is a global researcher and *New York Times* bestselling author focused on unlocking people's strengths, increasing their performance, and defining a better future for how people work. He is the author of two of the bestselling business books of all time, *First, Break All the Rules* (with Curt Coffman) and *Now, Discover Your Strengths* (with Donald O. Clifton). He wrote two of *Harvard Business Review*'s most circulated, industry-changing cover articles, and he cocreated the StrengthsFinder and StandOut strengths assessments, which have been taken by over ten million people worldwide. Today he's the cohead of the ADP Research Institute, where he leads studies into people and performance around the world.